new products and diversification

new products
and diversification

Peter M. Kraushar, M.A. *(Cantab.)*
Managing Director, D. & F. Marketing Development Limited

BRANDON/SYSTEMS PRESS, INC.
Princeton   New York   London

Copyright 1970 by Brandon/Systems Press, Inc.,
a subsidiary of Brandon Applied Systems, Inc.
First published 1969 by Business Books Ltd.

contents

plates

introduction

New product development and diversification are subjects which are now recognized to be vital to the future of companies. The government, too, have realized the importance of general innovation by industry at large and its effects on the competitiveness of U.K. industry in world markets.

I have also found that these are fascinating subjects in which every executive is very interested and generally holds strong views. The very mention of development is enough to start a discussion on why some new products fail and others succeed, the best organization for development, etc.

Yet whenever I am asked to recommend a book on the subject which deals specifically with U.K. experience, I am always at a loss, because as far as I know no such book exists. I have dared to put pen to paper, therefore, in an attempt to satisfy this market gap.

My credentials lie in the work and experience of D & F Marketing Development Limited, as we claim to have been the first marketing group in the U.K. to specialize in this area in 1961 and since then have worked on over 300 projects for many leading U.K. and international companies. I have tried to draw on our experience as much as possible, because I believe that in development and diversification, as in many aspects of business, there is a strong divergence between theory and practice and it is useless to draw up very sophisticated models or complicated mathematical 'solutions' if no one can understand them or has the time to use them. For example, a mathematical approach to development, though it had achieved some success in the United States, failed to find a single buyer in the U.K., because a company's management did not have enough faith to be guided in important investment decisions by an answer given by a computer at the end of a process which only an experienced mathematician could begin to understand. Who can blame the management for not trying?

At the same time, I have resisted the temptation of looking at all our projects in order to derive some statistical data from them.

One of the main lessons I have learned about development lies in the differences rather than the similarities between companies, so statistics can be misleading and I have tried to use the experience in a qualitative sense instead.

It would be unrealistic to expect that such a book can provide answers to specific development problems. There is no magic formula to success in development and each individual or each company concerned will need to find its own path to that goal. I hope, however, that this book will provide general information to all those interested in the topic and a background to those actually involved in this field which they will be able to adapt to their own circumstances. It should also be particularly suitable to advanced students of marketing and of business in general.

In many cases the reader may feel that I am simply stating the obvious. If this is so, I apologize, but my excuse is that so often even large and sophisticated companies are terribly inefficient in development and diversification and the most obvious points are rarely put into practice.

I have concentrated on consumer rather than on industrial goods because my experience is mainly with the former. Much of the approach can be adapted for industrial goods, but I do not believe that the two categories can be covered satisfactorily in one book.

My thanks go to the companies and to my colleagues with whom I have discussed every aspect of development and diversification over many years. And to the Baker Library at Harvard for having such a splendid collection of U.S. books on marketing subjects, of which I availed myself while on an International Marketing Institute course there. Finally, I must thank my wife to whom this book is dedicated. Over the last year she must have thought that she had married a book rather than a husband.

London, July 1968.

one the need for new products or for diversification

definition

The term 'new product' can cover a multitude of sins:

1 small changes to an existing brand such as new packaging, new sizes or the addition of new varieties.
2 major innovations in a company's existing markets.
3 a product similar or identical to one already being marketed by a competitor, but in a market new to the company concerned.
4 a product different from any being marketed in the same country, but already existing abroad.
5 a product which is different from any marketed by anyone anywhere, i.e. a true innovation.

My own definition covers categories 2, 3, 4, and 5 above. Moreover it includes new products which a company obtains from acquisition, as well as those resulting from Research and Development activity within the company. Acquisitions are normally treated separately from new product development, but there is a close connection between the two approaches to innovation or diversification, so it is important to look at both together.

awareness of need

Even a few years ago, certainly in the early 1950's, many companies did not think that new products were necessary to them. Their growth had been based often on one or two products which had perhaps played a predominant role in the company's history, e.g. sugar for Tate and Lyle, tea for Brooke Bond, chocolate for Cadbury's, stout for Guinness, bicycles for Raleigh, and it did not seem to make sense that a satisfactory profit position should be jeopardized by going in for new things, often in fields in which the company would have little or no experience.

Since then, however, the situation has changed completely. In the late 1950's and early 1960's the importance of new products became recognized to such an extent that it is never challenged today. In fact it is difficult to find recent quotations on this matter, probably because it is now felt that they would be no more than platitudes, repeating an established fact.

Some of the earlier statements were interesting. In 1960 a Nielsen survey showed that in the United States 47 per cent of fast-moving consumer goods audited by them represented brands launched since 1950. In 1964 the deputy chairman of the U.K. Campbell Soup Company estimated that by 1974 up to 80 per cent of grocery trade turnover would come from new products not existing at the time. Also in 1964 Nielsen reported that over half of consumer spending on packaged detergents was on products launched after 1950. In France it was estimated by Leduc[1] that 73 per cent of the detergent market was held by brands launched in the previous eight years. In 1965 J. Walter Thompson[2] analysed a sample of U.K. product categories from grocery price lists between 1954 and 1964. It was estimated that of the 534 company names listed in 1964 in the 29 categories covered over half had entered these fields since 1954. Prof. Pessemier[3] estimates that in 1965 3 per cent of the gross national product (G.N.P.) was devoted in the United States to the development of new products and services—more than double the expenditure in 1957. R. and D. expenditure in the U.K. has similarly shot up

[1]. *How to Launch a New Product*, R. Leduc, Crosby, Lockwood and Son Limited, 1966.
[2]. *New Lamps for Old*, J. Walter Thompson Company Limited, 1965.
[3]. *New Product Decisions — An Analytical Approach*, Prof. E. Pessemier, McGraw Hill, 1968.

and is currently estimated at 2.3 per cent of G.N.P., above Holland, France, Germany, Japan, Sweden and Canada, and is growing at some 10 per cent per annum.

Thus the case for innovation seems proved and nearly every company accepts it. Brooke Bond have diversified into coffee, food broking, cheese, spices, meat, data processing and even travel. Tate and Lyle announced in December 1967 the formation of a new company for diversification, Guinness have moved into lager, pharmaceuticals and confectionery, while Raleigh announced in 1968 entry into the pram market. I have discussed personally the matter of innovation with over two hundred consumer goods companies in the period 1966–68 and not one challenged the need for new products.

Companies now realize that they must innovate not only to increase their profits but even to maintain them. The accelerating rate of technological innovation coupled with increasing competition have been leading to shorter life cycles for existing products. And, as the chairman of the Board of Du Pont [1] said in 1963: 'Lead time is gone. There is no company so outstanding technically today that it can expect a long lead in a new discovery'.

It may be sad, but the destiny for a product must be eventual death, though the actual length of the life cycle obviously varies a great deal, so if a company wants to live it must innovate and it is interesting that, in the United States at any rate, a company's product development record has become one of the main factors by which a company is assessed by investment analysts.[2]

product life cycles

Nielsen [3] recently produced some useful evidence on the life cycles of new products, based on the investigation of 454 grocery brands from 35 product categories in the United States

1. *Time,* March 29, 1963.
2. *Management of New Products,* Booz, Allen and Hamilton, 1964.
3. *The Nielsen Researcher Oxford Edition,* May/June, 1967.

and from 39 product categories in Britain during the period 1961–66. Nielsen defined as a brand's primary cycle the period from a brand's initial growth up to the time when its share fell below 80 per cent of the first crest. On this basis 54 per cent of the new brands had a primary cycle lasting under two years and only 13 per cent continued to grow after three years.

The U.S. section of the study also clearly showed the expected decrease in the length of the primary cycle as markets have become increasingly competitive over the years. In the product categories covered the median length of primary cycles was three years in 1962 and only eighteen months in 1964.

Finally an important number of brands were subjected to a recycle following the primary cycle, i.e. strong marketing action was taken once the brands had been shown to decline, and 40 per cent of the recycles included product innovation. It is noteworthy, however, that the average length of a recycle was only fifteen months and was becoming shorter each succeeding year covered by the study.

The above findings clearly illustrate how terrifyingly short a product's life cycle is becoming, certainly in the case of recently introduced products, though it must be borne in mind that this aspect would have been exaggerated by Nielsen's concentration on fast-moving grocery products.

It is also to be noted that the Nielsen data apply only to products introduced recently. It is possible and indeed it is likely that the life cycle of a new product these days is very short and is becoming shorter all the time, whereas the picture is very different in the case of the old-established products. If this is so, it is an important point closely related to the need for new products in companies which possess some old-established ones.

For example, there is no sign that products such as Bisto, Bovril, Guinness, Dettol, Horlicks, Ovaltine and many others of this vintage are declining or dying. Whatever should be happening to them on a life-cycle basis, these products are not only alive but they are prospering and in general increasing turnover and profits over the year.

It is easy to be frightened regarding the future of a company's products even if they are healthy and prospering. For example, Theodore Levitt's famous article 'Marketing Myopia'[1] had a salutary effect when first published in showing how companies do not innovate in their own fields through having too narrow a view of them—the U.S. railways should have thought that they were not in rail but in transport and so should have gone into air transport—but this argument is now used to persuade companies to diversify at all cost. Yet timing is vital and there is certainly some evidence that companies should not be too pessimistic regarding the time-span within which an old-established product will continue to be profitable.

Moreover, I believe that there is considerable room for improvement in extending life cycles if the company plans accordingly. For example, if it is accepted that a new product

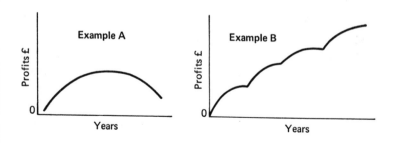

will be declining after, say, three years and nothing is done until the decline sets in, the company deserves the failure it probably has on its hands. If, on the other hand, this factor is taken into account before the product is launched, it may be possible to build ingredients into the product and its marketing which will allow it to extend its cycle at the critical points. Thus the profit pattern can be transformed from the pattern shown in example A to that in example B.

Such cycle extension may sound highly theoretical, but in fact

1. 'Marketing Myopia,' *Harvard Business Review*, July/August, 1960.

has taken place a number of times and Theodore Levitt[1] has described three successful cases—Nylon, General Foods' Jell-O and Minnesota Mining and Manufacturing Company's 'Scotch' Tape. In all three cases the companies had planned an extension of either the product's number of users or of its actual uses at critical points. In practice on a number of occasions when the growth pattern was beginning to fail, the companies were completely successful in putting their plans in operation.

In the case of nylon, Du Pont extended its use first into other types of hosiery—highly patterned and coloured stockings—and then into new product categories such as carpets, tyres, etc. Similarly, Jell-O extended its cycle first by adding new varieties, then by extending its uses to salads and finally by finding new users—weight watchers—and by finding completely new uses for the basic gelatine.

It is this kind of planning which can make the difference between success and relative failure. Nylon is still going strong but, as Levitt says, this would not have happened if new uses had not been found for the same basic material. There were danger points in its growth in 1945, 1948, 1955 and 1959 and decline could well have set in at these points, but each time Du Pont had a trick up its sleeve.

Nevertheless, however sophisticated the company may be in dealing with life cycles, it seems reasonable to believe that products finally really do decline and die and companies need to plan continually to develop new products to add to and eventually to supersede the existing ones.

but are new products automatic salvation?

An existing product must eventually die. The rate of change is accelerating. Life cycles are becoming shorter and shorter. A company's salvation must lie in new products. The case seems proved.

1. 'Market Stretching', Theodore Levitt, *Marketing*, June, 1966.

Yet in real life the situation is not so simple. The importance of new products is so well known now in most companies that this thinking has actually become dangerous to many, because new products have become manna from heaven, the answer to every problem. This attitude can lead to a new disease, 'new product hysteria', resulting in quick acquisitions or new product launches which, if unsuccessful, can inhibit the company's progress for a long time, not only in financial terms but also by putting up psychological barriers against future innovation. How many companies there are with such a go/stop policy, launching in too much of a hurry and then being afraid of doing anything else for ten years!

If I sound over-pessimistic, let us look at some facts. How many successes have been launched in the U.K. in the last ten years? Although no exact figures are available, there are some useful indications. William Ramsay, Development Manager of Alfred Bird (now General Foods) looked in April 1967 [1] at major grocery brands launched in the U.K. in the period 1956–65. He classified these as having annual sales of at least £1m. at retail selling price (R.S.P.) and on the basis of Nielsen data estimated that only 25 products launched since 1956 had achieved the £1m. mark. These only represented between 15 per cent and 20 per cent of all grocery products retailing at over £1m.

Even if the figures above are underestimates—I believe that the correct number of new major grocery brands is between 30 and 35—this figure is still astonishingly low. Moreover the new major brands are on average likely to be smaller in turnover than the old established brands, so the percentage of turnover of all major brands accounted for by the new ones is probably in the region of 15 per cent. Perhaps new products are not the automatic solution to every problem. The figures above certainly deserve much reflection.

What about acquisitions? How have they fared? Here it is even more difficult to give a definite answer, but there are again indications that many are unsuccessful (see page 197). This view is supported by a recent study conducted in the

1. *Financial Times*, April 12, 1967.

United States by John Kitching.[1] He covered the acquisition policy of 20 U.S. companies and examined in detail 69 acquisitions which they had made at least two years before the survey. Nineteen were considered failures and 3 others were considered failures at first, but were later turned into successes. In general he felt that the top executives interviewed were unhappy about their companies' acquisition activities, being particularly uneasy about the high degree of risk involved which was so difficult to quantify when compared with other forms of investment.

In my experience, the findings described above would certainly apply to the U.K. to an even greater extent, because there is no doubt that U.S. companies are ahead in sophisticated techniques designed to appraise acquisitions.

If, however, it is so difficult to innovate or diversify, is it better not to try? Have the arguments advanced earlier in this book gone overboard? The answer is no, definitely not. I draw four main conclusions:

1 Companies must have a balanced attitude towards new products and acquisitions. They must not regard them as automatic solutions to their problems. It is important, therefore, that every effort be made to optimize first the results from the company's existing products so that, if the company decides to embark on the uncharted waters of innovation or diversification, it does so with a solid, well-manned ship.

2 Innovation need not be the most profitable course for every company. It is possible that in some cases the shareholders' interests are best served, certainly in the short and medium term, by a conscious decision to concentrate on the existing products without any innovation apart from minor product improvements.

3 In the long term, however, a company's future must lie in innovation. Otherwise, however good its products, it will

1. 'Why Do Mergers Miscarry?', J. Kitching, *Harvard Business Review*, November/December 1967.

be caught out by the competition just as Henry Ford was caught by General Motors because of his persistence with his Model T.

A company should certainly seek new products, but this should be done with a real understanding of the risks involved. It is necessary, therefore, for a company to adopt an organization, a set of procedures and an attitude of mind which are appropriate to the opportunities and the risks presented by new products.

The need for new products is very real, but the need to understand the implications is as important.

4 Innovation must not be confused with diversification. Companies can be most successful by limiting their operations to a very restricted field, so long as they are prepared to innovate in order to defend their long-term future in that field. For example, it is believed that Wrigley's policy is to restrict themselves to chewing gum, in which they are dominant internationally, and this approach has been very successful and profitable.

Diversification into new fields probably presents greater opportunities, but also has far greater risks. The decision whether a company should diversify or just innovate in its current fields is probably the most important one that it needs to take and the relative advantages and disadvantages of the two approaches deserve very detailed examination. In my experience this rarely happens.

some company histories

It is instructive to look at a number of companies in relation to their new product development and diversification activities.

a) THE CADBURY GROUP

The company is an old-established chocolate manufacturer with two of the major brands in the U.K. market, Cadbury's and Fry's. The market has become relatively static and it has proved particularly difficult for all companies in it to introduce major new products successfully.

Since 1962 the company has been exploring new markets and has diversified into cakes, biscuits, Christmas puddings, meat processing, vending machines, instant potato and prepared desserts. The sales and profit record has been as follows:

	Sales	Profits	Return on capital
	£m.	£m.	%
1957	83	8·0	18
1958	84	8·5	16
1959	85	7·4	14
1960	87	9·0	15
1961	92	8·8	14
1962	94	8·6	13
1963	96	8·7	12
1964	102	7·7	10
1965	115	9·5	12
1966	131	10.6	13
1967	137	9·8	11

Although it would be wrong to relate the company's results to development activity alone, it seems clear that until diversification took place profits were static and return on capital dropped while turnover rose very slowly. Recently, however, turnover has risen substantially but profits and return on capital have certainly not followed the same pattern. In fact the Cadbury results so far are typical of a company deciding to diversify. Expensive failures have inevitably taken place, e.g. the venture into meat processing, but the success likely to result from instant milk, cakes and instant potato should improve the profit picture and the return on capital in the next few years.

b) NESTLE ALIMENTANA S.A.

Having started from a condensed milk factory in 1866, Nestlé began to market such products as coffee with milk, cocoa with milk, chocolate with milk and cheese as well as condensed milk. In 1904 it acquired an interest in chocolate and later distributed even butter. In 1938 Nescafé was launched and after the Second World War it was relaunched internationally, soon followed by Nesquick and Nestea. In 1947 the merger took place with Maggi and in 1960 with Crosse and Black-well, thus extending the Nestlé interests into such products as cubes, packet soups, canned soups, pickles, canned peas, beans, fish and marmalade. Soon afterwards, Nestlé entered the ice cream market through agreement with French, German, Austrian and Spanish companies and the next logical step was an entry into the frozen food market by acquiring Findus together with the Swedish company, A/B Marabou. The recent trading picture has been as follows:

	Sales	Assets	Net Profit
	$m.	$m.	$m.
1960	1,281	225	15
1961	1,519	239	20
1962	1,628	256	20
1963	1,829	275	22
1964	1,448	324	24
1965	1,563	357	28
1966	1,703	383	30

Although the advance has not been spectacular, this seems a good example of a company which has pursued, particularly since the war, a policy of vertical and horizontal integration in the food market to reach the position of a giant in the food field. Presumably the power this will give Nestlé will be an important competitive benefit in the future and the most recent results indicate that the growth rate is already accelerating.

c) PILLSBURY

Pillsbury started as a flour milling concern in Minnesota in 1869. Until the Second World War it confined its activities to grain, flour and bakery interests in the United States and

Canada. In 1960, however, it began to diversify and has since made numerous acquisitions such as household cleaning products (U.S.), baked goods, pasta and confectionery (France), frozen foods (U.S.A.), retailing (Australia), tinned goods and chocolate (Germany), bakery products and flour mixes (U.K.), restaurants (U.S.).

In addition Pillsbury has undertaken a vigorous programme of new product development by launching such products as cake mixes, frozen foods, cyclamate products, drink mixes, broiler chickens. The effect of the new policy on sales and profits is noteworthy.

	Sales	Profits
	$m.	$m.
1946	140	4
1947	188	9
1948	226	6
1949	200	3
1950	200	2
1951	224	5
1952	314	8
1953	336	10
1954	335	11
1955	341	12
1956	330	11
1957	331	10
1958	350	14
1959	359	19
1960	373	15
1961	384	19
1962	398	17
1963	407	16
1964	446	20
1965	443	23
1966	470	25

Turnover had been almost static between 1952 and 1959, but has risen steadily since. The profit picture is more erratic, clearly reflecting setbacks as well as investment, yet the general trend is again strongly upwards. Moreover, having become a very diversified company, Pillsbury must be facing the future with more confidence from its wide base than it would if it still had to depend almost entirely on flour and flour products.

d) TATE AND LYLE

Tate and Lyle is a company which has diversified very little, marketing only sugar and sugar by-products such as rum and syrup. There has also been little scope for innovation among its present products.

Its sales have been as follows:

	Sales
	£m.
1957	155
1958	129
1959	140
1960	135
1961	116
1962	120
1963	125
1964	144
1965	141
1966	125

The company seems to have reached a plateau in turnover which in fact was lower in 1966 than in 1957. Its profits in the last few years show a slightly different pattern having been as follows:

	Profits
	£m.
1961	7·3
1962	6·9
1963	9·5
1964	8·7
1965	8·7
1966	7·4
1967	9·5

Even though there has been a short term profit revival, 1967 profits were no higher than in 1963 and the company does seem vulnerable because of its complete dependence on sugar. For example, it could be seriously affected by the recent U.K. legislation allowing the use of cyclamate as sugar substitute in foods starting from December 1967. It is not surprising that it has announced its intention to diversify by forming a new company specifically for this purpose.

e) GUINNESS

Guinness is an example of a company which owes its success to one product and has been somewhat unsuccessful in trying to diversify. It has ventured into lager, confectionery and pharmaceuticals, but of its new ventures only lager has so far been proved financially promising.

Its record has been as follows:

	Profits before tax	% on capital employed
	£m.	%
1958	8·2	26
1959	7·4	23
1960	8·2	23
1961	8·0	21
1962	7·8	18
1963	8·4	19
1964	9·3	20
1965	8·6	18
1966	9·7	19
1967	11·1	21

The company is clearly raising its profit levels and its return on capital is also improving, though it is below its pre-1960 levels. Harp Lager is known to have been successful and in 1967 brought Guinness profits of £506,000. The pharmaceutical diversification, however, has not been profitable so far. Losses in 1967 were over £1m. and were similar to those in 1966. The Nuttall confectionery group (part of Guinness) has also been disappointing, though it has generated some profit.

It can be seen, therefore, that most of the company's diversification activities have impeded growth, which would have been better if the company had concentrated on marketing Guinness and Harp Lager.

two new product failures

rate of failures

Some new products fail and some succeed. But what is failure?
What is success? How many fail? How many succeed? Why?

There are no satisfactory answers to the above questions,
mainly because yet again the problem of definition is intract-
able. Not only is there the usual difficulty in defining a new
product—every one uses different definitions—but also what
would be a failure to one company could be a success to another. Moreover failure rate figures are applied to products in
various stages of development. Some talk in terms of the percentage of new ideas which lead to one success. Others estimate
the failure rate of products placed into test market.

It follows, therefore, that the wealth of information which
exists on the failure rate of new products needs to be treated
with care. The Shering Drug Company of New Jersey, for
example, estimated in 1966 that they had screened 13,500
antibiotics during the previous year. Of these, 350 looked
active and 16 seemed worth looking at, being different from
existing products. Finally 5 were shortlisted and the company
believed that one of them had a 33 per cent chance of being
marketed. N. H. Borden Jr.[1] quoted in his doctoral thesis
various estimates on the proportion of new items offered to
U.S. supermarkets which had in fact been accepted. A buyer
from American Stores had estimated the figure at 977 out of
4,303. Allied Supermarkets had considered 3,696 new items

1. *The Introduction of New Products to Supermarkets.* Doctoral Thesis at
Harvard Business School. N. H. Borden Jr., December, 1964.

over a twelve months' period and had accepted 756. In addition, many others had not been considered. *Progressive Grocer* estimated that 6,000 new items had been offered to a typical U.S. supermarket during 1961 and about 300 had been accepted.

In 1955 the New Product Institute Incorporated published the results of research among 200 large manufacturers of packaged consumer items in the United States who had introduced new products since 1945. All the companies were extremely successful and prosperous and had large resources to support the development and launch of new products. Yet, when asked about the success rate of new product launches, these 200 companies claimed that only 19 per cent of the products placed on the market in the previous few years had been successful. The majority (77 per cent) also claimed that their competitors had been even less successful, although one cannot imagine that bias would be absent from such an answer!

It is a pity that most of the evidence on the failure rate comes from the United States rather than from the U.K., although the indications are that the pattern in the two countries is similar. In the U.K. Nielsen[1] analysed the results of forty-four new grocery products launched into test market over a fourteen year period. Almost half went on to national marketing—a similar proportion to that calculated by Nielsen in the U.S. in 1962. The 1965 J. Walter Thompson study of entries in grocery price lists showed that of the 402 products in fields new to their companies which had been entered between 1955 and 1963, 41 per cent no longer existed in 1964 and presumably many others were still on sale but had failed. The small number of major new grocery products introduced in the U.K. in the period 1956–65, as mentioned on page 7, must support the theory of the high failure rate, because there has certainly been no lack of major new product launches in this period.

It seems pointless, in my opinion, to explore the failure rate further because it is impossible to established an accurate figure and it does not matter whether the rate is 90 per cent,

1. *How to strengthen Your Product Plan*, A. C. Nielsen Company, 1966.

80 per cent or even 70 per cent. What is important is to establish certain general conclusions:

1 A very large number of new product ideas are necessary at the initial stage for weeding out through subsequent stages if a successful product is to be achieved at the end of the process.

2 Even when a new product is produced and marketed, a large proportion fail—well over half. I am convinced that the Nielsen failure rate after test market is an underestimate for two main reasons:
   a the companies using Nielsen tend to be above average in marketing expertise and so are likely to do much more pre-testing than the average company.
   b It is not possible to define a success or failure accurately without knowledge of the profit figures. It is common to see companies launching new products after test market though the test market indicates failure. Alternatively a product successful in test market may for various reasons become unprofitable in national marketing. Yet any product launched nationally after test market would have been included by Nielsen in the successful category.

It should be accepted, therefore, that new product development is a hazardous business, whatever the failure rate. What is more rewarding and useful than study of the failure rate is analysis of actual failures to establish whether there are any general principles which can be applied.

some failures

A study of product failures over the last fifteen years shows that a very large number have taken place, although it is difficult to obtain information about them as most companies are keener to shout about their successes than about their failures.

The Edsel disaster in the United States, despite Ford's meticulous research programme, is very well known. In fact, almost every important consumer goods manufacturer, however experienced and sophisticated in marketing methods, has one or more skeletons locked in the new product disaster cupboard.

Unilever, for example, lost a great deal of money in launching Spree—a squash concentrate packed in small sachets. There seemed to be little demand for the product at a price which was very high in relation to the usual squash bottle.

I.C.I. recently launched a range of do-it-yourself products designed to break into the Polycell franchise in this field, which seem to have met with little success despite the considerable effort put behind this venture.

Beechams has had its failures. *Advertising in Action*[1] describes how a shampoo was developed with a new method of application. After a successful test market, it was launched nationally with very heavy advertising and became the brand leader within six months. The fall was nearly as rapid because the novelty wore off and the public returned to the conventional products. In fact the shampoo market has been a graveyard for new products, as women have been found willing to experiment, but fickle in continuing brand loyalty.

Meat products are another market where many companies have tried and later wished that they had not. Crosse and Blackwell, Cadbury's, Dalgety and Schweppes are among these. The market is certainly attractive because of its size and at first sight there should be much opportunity for branded convenience products. The important price sensitivity, however, in this commodity market, combined with the difficulty of packaging meat dishes of a quality matching the promise of the surface design on the pack, has proved too much for most of the entrants. By contrast, the success of Vesta and of Fray Bentos shows what could have been achieved.

There have been several interesting cases of two or more companies launching similar products and meeting with very different success. A good example was the launch of Frutips

1. *Advertising in Action*, Ralph Harris and Arthur Seldon, Hutchinson, 1962.

by Nestlé, a range of chewy sweets which was almost the same as Opal Fruits launched by Mars at the same time. Opal Fruits went on to be one of the more successful new confectionery lines whereas Frutips soon failed. Why? The main difference was not between the products—both were very acceptable to the public—or between the marketing methods. I believe that the main difference lay in the suitability of the market to the two companies. Mars was very much more of a 'sweet' company than Nestlé from the point of view of both the trade and the public and had previously introduced other successful lines. Therefore, other things being equal, it was much easier for Mars than for Nestlé to launch such a product. Likewise it would have been much more difficult for Mars to launch a tinned cream product than it was for Nestlé, whose Nestlé's Cream has been one of the more successful food products in the U.K. after the war.

The chocolate and sugar confectionery market has in fact been one of the most difficult ones for new products. There is some similarity with the shampoo market as here again the consumer seeks variety and is very happy to try new products, but is rarely satisfied with them for long. Thus the market is mostly dominated by lines which have been in existence for many years despite all the efforts at innovation by the main manufacturers. A good example of a promising new line was Mackintosh's Caramac, a chocolate bar which achieved immediate success until the public became weary of it.

The slimming remedy market has been another where products have been launched with high hopes, to be quashed as the public refused to continue to buy the products regularly. Largely on the basis of U.S. trends it was expected that this market would become very large, but this has not happened and Mead Johnson's Metercal was only one of a score of such products which were extremely disappointing. Similarly, men's toiletries were expected to grow to U.S. levels and there were again crashing failures, including Beecham's Mark Vardy range. It is interesting, however, that in recent years the market has continued to grow, though much more modestly than expected and timing may have been an important factor in the failures. The products may have been launched too early for the market.

Timing is clearly an important factor, and yet it is so difficult to judge in advance whether a product is too early for its market or not. Malling[1] quotes the Chrysler Airflow design of 1934 as 8–10 years too early. The Edsel's failure was probably due to bad timing. General Electric marketed the 'V' wire wound resistor which was hailed by everyone at first and was a terrible failure – it was too late.

In the U.K. Birds Eye has tried to launch frozen orange juice a number of times and each time results have been disappointing because we are still far behind the U.S. in our breakfast habits and in our possession of refrigerators and freezers. It may be a success in a few years' time. Nestea was an important failure for Nestlé despite the very large expenditure behind it. The failure was mainly attributed to the British teamaking ritual, yet this has now been disturbed by tea bags and instant tea may well be acceptable in the years to come.

Instant potato products are a good example of different rates of acceptance due to timing. In the early 1960's Bibby, Batchelor and Mars tested instant potato products with considerable backing, but the results were poor. Since then the market has slowly expanded until recently, when Mars launched a second product to complement its existing brand. Cadbury's entered the market, so did Ranks Hovis McDougall and everyone else looked on with interest at a very fast-expanding market which suddenly had become completely different from that seven years before.

Dishwashers are yet another category which has been disappointing in the U.K. so far, mainly because of bad timing. Over the last five or six years it has been often said that the breakthrough would come and that, as the household's needs are becoming satisfied, the dishwasher would be the next appliance to turn to. This has certainly not happened so far,

1. *Marketing Timing*, E. A. Malling, Management Research and Development Institute, Crotonville, N.Y.

probably because of the repeated restrictions which consumer expenditure has been suffering.

It still seems likely, however, that this is one of the appliances of the future and it is not surprising that most appliance manufacturers have a model ready to launch when the time is ripe. In fact Hoover launched their model recently and probably increased further the industry's interest in dishwashers.

Price in relation to the product has often been the cause of failure. A number of aerosol products have failed badly, e.g. aerosol shoe polishes, because the extra convenience has not outweighed the high price. The failure of Whoosh, the chocolate milk drink in an aerosol, can again be attributed to this reason, whereas on the other hand aerosol oven cleansers have been a reasonable success because the housewife obviously thinks it is worthwhile to pay a considerable premium to lighten the nasty chore of cleaning her oven.

Harvey's of Bristol probably found an important opportunity in the launch of a range of branded wines to be distributed nationally under the name of Club No. 1. Unfortunately the price at which it was marketed was too high for the mass market seeking the reassurance of a national brand and they continued to drink the cheaper wines, however inferior. The opportunity in branded wines has been confirmed by the success of branded Mateus and the current interest of all the major brewery groups in this market sector is likely to develop it and to establish a number of important brands at the expense of the many small ones currently on the market.

Procter and Gamble's Cheer was another product to bite the dust because of price. A detergent with a duster enclosed in each pack, it was priced above other detergents and housewives showed that the higher price did not compensate for all the dusters. Kayser Bondor's venture into children's clothes met a similar fate. They were expensive, though of high quality, and did not meet the mother's demand for low-priced clothes for children who wear out their clothes so fast.

Failure may stem from prices that are too low as well as from those that are too high. I know of at least two products launched by very large companies at an incorrect price, so that the more that was sold the greater the loss. Not surprisingly, they were both withdrawn. Pricing was also a factor in the staggering success and in the equally staggering failure of Rolls washing machines. The very low prices meant that extremely high turnover and tight financial control were essential for success. When the turnover fell and the financial control seemingly was not as tight as it might have been, failure was inevitable.

Many failures can be attributed to one general reason, i.e. to a wrong product. Either the product does not perform adequately or it is not significantly different from existing products or, even if it is different, there is no dissatisfaction with existing products which would lead the public to switch to a new product. Thus General Mills' Betty Crocker cake mixes were a complete failure in the U.K. because the products were unsuitable for the British market. Fluoride toothpastes, on the other hand, have certainly obtained some acceptance as well as much professional approval, but the British public have not been impressed enough to give up traditional toothpaste despite marketing of fluoride by Gibbs and Colgate. Thus the share of fluoride toothpastes is still unexpectedly low and it is noteworthy that Procter and Gamble decided not to launch Crest Fluoride nationally after prolonged testing.

Karwad, Reckitts' car polish in a pad, was another failure —a product which the public did not seem to want—while General Foods have tried more than once to launch Jell-O in the U.K. and again found that there was no demand for it in this country. Similarly, fabric softeners which have achieved significant levels of acceptance in the United States have been marketed by a number of companies in the U.K. with signal lack of success so far. Despite considerable expenditure on advertising designed to 'educate' the British housewife, so far she has not been persuaded of the usefulness of yet another type of laundry product.

Possibly the most mysterious failures lie in the tobacco field.

A mass of cigarette brands have failed over the years, Kingsway, Olivier, Bristol, Everest, Admiral, Viscount, etc., yet no one really knows why one brand fails and another succeeds. Communication of a suitable image is probably the main factor which makes a cigarette the right or the wrong product for the market.

reasons for failure

The examples already mentioned in this chapter show various reasons for failure. The 1966 Nielsen study of 44 failures[1] shows that the following reasons were advanced for failure:

	Main reason	All reasons
	%	%
Product/Package	53	35
Price/Value	20	19
Trade acceptance	18	29
Advertising	9	17
	100	100

Thus the main reason for failure seems to lie in an unacceptable product or pack, while price and lack of trade acceptance were also notable factors. Closer study of eight failures considered by Nielsen shows that they tended to be competitive in price and in marketing support, but few presented a new product idea, none stood out with regard to product quality and in general the distribution levels achieved were low.

The importance of the product itself as the main cause of failure seems inescapable.

When the 200 large U.S. manufacturers were asked by the New Products Institute (see page 16) what were the greatest causes of failure, the replies included such factors as lack of a well thought out marketing programme, lack of pre-testing, lack of market test, impatience, insufficient planning and pre-

1. *How To Strengthen Your Product Plan*, A. C. Nielsen Company Limited, 1966.

paration, lack of understanding of the market, lack of the necessary time and resources to launch successfully.

These are all valid points. They are also very simple factors and I find it surprising that large and sophisticated companies, well-staffed with marketing executives, can have failures for reasons which would often be apparent to the most junior marketing assistant. How can a company risk a large expenditure in the 1960's without knowing what the consumer thinks of the product? How can a company not bother to obtain a feel of the market? How can a company aim for long-term investment in a market known for its fickleness and absence of continuous brand loyalty? How can a company launch a new product these days which is found to be unacceptable by the consumer?

I am convinced that there is one general answer which goes some way to explain this strange phenomenon. The answer is largely *lack of objectivity*.

A company is subject to many pressures. Personal pressures, political pressures, financial pressures, 'action' pressures, etc. The chairman may have a stream of new product ideas and it is difficult to say 'no' every time. The idea develops, from whatever source, and after a certain stage it is difficult to stop it. Everyone becomes enthusiastic, the profit and loss forecasts look good. No wonder that everyone wants the new project to succeed and so it is pushed along and, if by any chance research shows that there are snags, these are minimized and all possible extenuating reasons are invoked for going on. It is unpopular to say 'no'.

Moreover it is not easy for a company to be objective enough to look at itself and see both its strength and its weaknesses. I am sure that there is no such thing as a good or a bad opportunity—it is only good or bad according to the company concerned—and many of the failures suggest that one company can succeed where another fails and vice versa. If this is accepted, it is crucial that a company should examine itself closely to determine what type of market it is most suitable to enter. Yet companies find such introversion difficult and so choose wrong markets. For example, a number of industrial companies in the U.K. have gone into consumer goods without relating the needs of these markets to their own skills and the results have on the whole been disastrous.

Such lack of objectivity would explain why many of the top companies act as they do. Top management press for action, an opportunity looks good on paper, the company profile is not considered, there is fear of the competition taking the same action. All these factors add up to a compulsive urge to go ahead unless there are strong negatives—and usually the reading is neither black nor white but grey, so interpretation makes it white. The product is launched. A few succeed. Many fail. And then one asks: 'How could such an obvious failure have been launched?'

The picture may seem grossly exaggerated and certainly there are companies where the dangers of lack of objectivity are now recognized and dealt with accordingly. In many large as well as small companies, however, such a situation persists and it is likely that we will see in the years ahead companies with the right organization and management attitude towards development streaking ahead of their less well-equipped competitors.

three new product successes

what is a success?

As usual, it is necessary to discuss definitions. What is a new product success?

There is no clear answer, unfortunately, except that it will vary according to the company. In theory, a new product is a success if it meets the company's development criteria. In practice, however, as these criteria so rarely exist, the new product is a success if the company's management just feel that the results are good. This feeling is probably subjective and empirical, yet it can work reasonably well, particularly if the company has launched a number of new products and so has past experience of the way in which they have performed at certain stages in their development.

However a company defines its new product successes, it is clear that what is a success for one company can be a failure for another, depending on the company—its resources, its attitudes, its plans, its criteria. Thus Golden Wonder crisps have probably proved a great success for Imperial Tobacco, having obtained about half the large and expanding U.K. crisp market. Imperial Tobacco, with its considerable resources and the need to diversify from tobacco products, must be gratified at the establishment of such a strong foothold in food. For many other companies, however, the long term investment which proved necessary would have meant that the project was a complete failure.

Similarly the advance made by Cadbury and by McVitie in the packaged cake market has received much publicity. Yet in both cases it is understood that by the middle of 1968 the success has been in terms of turnover only, as neither company has begun to run at a profit in this market. Whether the two ventures are in fact successes or not depends on the effort and on the investment that each of the two companies believes worthwhile in this particular case.

On the other hand, a new product yielding even £20,000–£30,000 profit from the first years, which is not capable of much growth from this level, could be a great success for a small company but a complete failure for a large one unable to afford to look after minor brands in case they take the sales force's attention away from the company's major profit earners.

It follows, therefore, that it is impossible to be accurate in calling a new product successful without actually sitting in the particular company's Boardroom. Nevertheless the attempt must be made and I will try to include as many undisputed successes as possible.

some new product successes

1. WILKINSON SWORD

There can be no doubt about the well known success of Wilkinson Sword razor blades. A relatively small family company, Wilkinson Sword made a technical breakthrough in developing a stainless steel blade of consistent quality. Not many would have given much for its chances against the experienced giant, Gillette, yet it proceeded to erode the latter's market share and to become a major force in the world's razor blade markets.

Gillette retaliated, as would be expected, by launching its own stainless steel product with considerable marketing expenditure, but in the ensuing battle Wilkinson Sword has still managed to retain some half of the U.K. market and, in addition, about 60 per cent of its current business is done overseas.

It is noteworthy that, although Wilkinson Sword markets a range of products, the success of the razor blade has completely changed the nature of the company which found itself almost overnight as an important force in a large consumer market and quickly adopted the attitudes and organization which one would expect in a large consumer goods company.

The success of Wilkinson Sword lies clearly in the product itself which had such strong advantages over the other razor blades when it was first launched that it established itself initially despite the lack of marketing support and of a large company organization.

2. HORIZON HOLIDAYS

After the war a Reuter correspondent, Vladimir Raitz, saw how much it cost to go by holiday by air if one used the usual scheduled flights and realized that there would be great possibilities for economy if aircraft were specially chartered for holidays to a particular resort.

This idea, which was first put into operation by Raitz who combined a charter flight with the offer of a tented holiday camp in Corsica, has now developed into the flourishing inclusive air holiday business. The principle remains the same, however, as the tour operator is able to offer holidays at very economical prices by booking hotels for the whole season and by chartering the planes. His profits are made according to his ability to fill the seats in these planes throughout the season.

Raitz's company, Horizon Holidays, has continued to play a leading role in the inclusive holiday market, though it has been overtaken in terms of size by a few competitors. Its success lies in the fact that, having originated the concept of inclusive air holidays, it has pursued a constant long-term policy of appealing to the middle-class market.

This policy has been reflected in the product itself. The actual resorts tend to be the less well-known places away from the waves of the tourist masses: the hotels are as carefully selected and controlled as possible in a field where quality control is extremely difficult, because a sudden change of a chef or of ownership can change a hotel from good to terrible and vice versa; the couriers on the spot are carefully instructed not to organize people's holidays unless there is demand for this; the prices tend to be higher than those of most inclusive air holidays.

The middle-class policy is translated into the literature and into the promotion for Horizon which, among the mass of holiday operators, all offering their wares in a concentrated period of time after Christmas each year, has managed to acquire and maintain a distinctive personality. It is known to offer holidays for the individualist who does not like to be shepherded around but who seeks the benefits of group discounts.

The above policy has disadvantages as well as advantages. By its nature it does not appeal to the mass market, particularly to those who want to be looked after all the time when they go abroad and it is probably for this reason that other companies have been more successful in attracting large numbers of holiday makers. Horizon's policy, however, has proved particularly profitable as it has thus avoided the pressures and the expenditure necessary in the mass holiday market.

It has also found itself insulated from the market fluctuations which have affected the general holiday market because of economic restrictions and has managed instead to grow at a steady rate every year.

3. TURTLE WAX POLISH

In 1960 Kilvert, a regional company manufacturing lard and suet with particular strength in Lancashire and Yorkshire,[1] was anxiously searching for new products and the managing director came across Turtle Wax car products on a visit to the United States, as one of a number of possibilities for diversification.

At first sight, nothing could appear more unlikely. Here was a relatively small food company without national distribution and without distribution in outlets other than grocers and yet it was interested in attacking a market of which it knew little, with completely different outlets, and which had a number of

1. *Case Studies in Marketing*, G. B. Giles, Macdonald and Evans Limited, July 1967.

established companies in it, including three leading U.S. companies—Simoniz, E. R. Howard and Johnson's.

It was found, however, that the Turtle Wax products were particularly effective and had been successful not only in the United States but also in Sweden through a local distributor. Kilvert decided, therefore, to test market the polish in this country, importing the product from the States and using a contract sales force. The product was priced at 12s 6d—more than the products on the market at the time—and the appeal to the consumer was that here was a high quality product to be used once a year. 12s 6d was not much to spend on a car once a year and, in fact, Kilvert could not charge less for the product because of the relatively high import and selling costs.

The test market was judged to be a success, distribution was expanded and other Turtle Wax products were added. Turtle Wax became an important factor in the U.K. car products market with leading shares in the polish and shampoo sectors.

This is a remarkable achievement if one bears in mind the handicaps under which Kilvert was operating. It seems, however, that a definite consumer need was met for a high quality product selling at a high price—the necessarily high price being translated into an advantage in this case.

4. ROLLS WASHING MACHINES

The failure of John Bloom's venture into low-priced washing machines is very well-known, but it should be appreciated that the eventual failure was probably due to faults in organization and in financial control which should not detract from what was in fact a striking success while it lasted.

The concept of by-passing the trade on a high-priced item and of going direct to the consumer by means of very heavy consumer advertising followed by door-to-door selling was simple and brilliant. It enabled Bloom to market a range of remarkably cheap washing machines and, starting from nothing, he soon achieved a large share of the U.K. market. As both the machines and the servicing facilities were of a good standard, so the reputation of the machines spread by word of mouth.

The selling operation depended on men relying on commission only and it attracted many high calibre men as the commission rates were extremely attractive. A number of professional men such as doctors and lawyers found it more exciting and profitable to sell washing machines and the efficiency of the door-to-door selling operation was, of course, a vital element in Bloom's success.

The growth of the operation was, therefore, due to a combination of factors:

1 The product—at least adequate.
2 The selling operation—most effective.
3 The marketing—concentration on advertising leading to economies in mass production.
4 The low price—resulting from the three factors above, and being the most important reason for Bloom's success in the absence of serious product negatives.

The Rolls operation had a profound effect on the consumer durable markets in this country and, quite apart from its own success, led to price cutting and to serious consideration of their marketing and distribution policies by the other appliance manufacturers. It was unfortunate that it went on to face financial problems which resulted in one of the greatest new product successes since the war finishing in liquidation.

5. PICKERINGS PIE FILLINGS

After the acquisition of Pickering and West, the Fison Group merged the new company with its existing food interests to form Fisons Foods. The new company faced an unpromising situation. Its business was mainly in canned fruit and canned vegetables sold on a contract basis through price deals. It had little experience of selling branded products except on price and its operation was regional, being concentrated in Lancashire and the Midlands.

It was in these difficult circumstances that Fisons Foods had the task of developing new branded products and a market they considered was that of tinned pie-fillings—a combination of fruit and starch which provides convenience over fresh fruit. The market had shown some buoyancy in the United States and in Canada, but in the U.K. it was still extremely small, consisting mainly of imported Canadian products with varieties which were not completely suitable to consumer habits in this country.

Fisons produced their own products under their Pickerings name, basing their range of varieties on the fillings used most often by British housewives in making pies at home. The products were tested, were then marketed in a couple of towns, went on to a television area, then to a region and finally after a lengthy step by step process the products were marketed nationally.

The gradual marketing approach enabled Fisons Foods to build up their sales and marketing organization to cope with national marketing and to deal with the competition which other companies, attracted by the way in which the market was growing, were likely to present.

In the event, Fisons quickly established dominance in the fast-growing market. Beechams and Robertsons both entered it spending on promotion at a much higher rate than Fisons, yet they only expanded the market while Fisons' share continued to rise, accounting by the beginning of 1968 for about half of the total market.

Thus Fisons not only managed to launch a successful new product in the fiercely competitive food market, but also built an organization to cope with national grocery marketing as the areas where the product was marketed were being expanded. No mean effort in the circumstances.

The product itself had some advantages over the ones in the market when it was launched. The varieties were right for British tastes and the quality was constant. Once it achieved its initial dominance, it probably benefited from the role of the innovator, being the first important brand in the market and this helped it in combating later competition.

An important factor in this context must have been the situation in the retail outlets. Although the market was growing, it was not large enough to support a number of important brands in the store and so the trade would naturally favour the market leader. Moreover there may have been some sympathy among the trade towards the small regional company fighting against much larger competitors. So again, other things being equal, Fisons would benefit.

The most important reason, however, for Fisons' success was the market itself. There was a definite market gap for providing convenience to housewives making pies and if only a small proportion used tinned pie-fillings this would result in a large enough market. Fisons exploited the market gap well and have certainly benefited from the results.

6. BIRDS EYE FROZEN FOODS

Following the development of quick-freezing by Clarence Birdseye in the 1920's, Unilever acquired in 1943 the manufacturing and selling rights for the process outside America, but were not able to launch any products till after the war.

Here again there was a clear market gap due to the high proportion of working wives requiring food products without much preparation and willing to pay a little more for the convenience so long as the quality was good.

The quick-freezing process would satisfy these needs in many cases, but it was essential for a large company to pioneer this market for the following reasons:

1 It was necessary to break down the consumer prejudices against convenience products which were very strong after the war, so it was essential to spend large sums on promotion to 'educate' the consumer.

2 Capital expenditure on plant and equipment was very large, both for manufacturing and for distribution. If prices were to bear any relationship to those of fresh food, it was necessary to seek economies of large scale produc-

tion, so it was not realistic to consider a small-scale operation. This factor again pointed to large expenditure on promotion to create mass consumer demand.

3 There were considerable problems with the trade, as it was important to persuade them of the potential for frozen food and to help them with the installation of expensive freezing cabinets.

4 Once a certain product range was established, it was necessary to investigate the possibilities of developing a very wide number of quick-frozen products, if the potential of the process was to be realized fully.

Few companies could have had the resources and the expertise shown by Unilever in carrying out such a project successfully. The growth of the frozen food market is well known and in this case the innovator could look to an ever greater prize than usual. The limited space in the freezing cabinet in a retail outlet must lead to above average stock concentration in favour of the market leader and so Birds Eye have made every effort to ensure that their initial market dominance would be maintained. In the event, they have continued to hold the bulk of the market, while competitors have found it hard to obtain important shares.

In this case early recognition of the market potential combined with good products and marketing policies which took advantage of Unilever's resources have led to a new product success which has had an important effect on the food industry in Britain and indeed in Europe.

7. BOOKS FOR PLEASURE

The U.K. publishing industry has been dominated by old-established companies selling through book outlets by means of traditional methods, regarding books as works of art rather than as products to be marketed to satisfy consumer demand.

Against such a background, Paul Hamlyn started by selling remainders and in a few years achieved important sales and profits for his company, Books for Pleasure, until he sold it to the International Publishing Corporation.

The secret of his new product success was that he did regard books as products designed for a certain market and he concentrated on well produced popular books which he managed to publish at very low prices through long runs, and particularly through printing in any country which offered the most economic rates. Thus many of the books were printed in Czechoslovakia at rates which would not have been possible in Britain.

By concentrating on popular subjects such as cookery and by giving considerable attention to the merchandising of the books in retail outlets, Hamlyn achieved sales levels which had been hitherto thought impossible by the publishing industry. Moreover, as outlets such as W. H. Smith found it necessary to rationalize on their stocks, the proven record for high turnover levels which had been established by Books for Pleasure meant that it did not suffer as the competition did.

In this case good products marketed at very low prices because of a completely new approach to book marketing led to success in a market which can still be regarded as production-oriented. It is noteworthy that recently Hamlyn has turned his attention to the gramophone record industry and his company, Records for Pleasure, is again achieving considerable success by marketing good quality recordings at low prices.

conclusions

If one considers the successes already described and other products and services which are known to have been successful in recent years, it is striking that much is due to the product itself. This sounds terribly obvious, but the general public often believe that advertising can sell anything, while many marketing experts have felt in the past that they can win by relying on huge financial resources and on superior marketing. This is probably the reason why so many U.S. products have failed in Britain since the war.

The need for a competitive product advantage does not

mean that a company needs to find a technological break-through, as Wilkinson Sword or Birds Eye did, before launch-ing a new product. Otherwise very few new products would ever be launched. It does mean, however, that good marketing and advertising are not enough or, at any rate, are very expen-sive in producing results if the product itself does not have a significant consumer benefit. This benefit could be in the pro-duct itself, e.g. Wilkinson Sword, in the price (Rolls Washing Machines, Books for Pleasure), in its packaging, or in the way in which it is distributed to the consumer.

For example, the Thomson publication, *Family Circle*, owes much of its success to its distribution through supermar-kets but even so it would not have been successful if the con-tents—concentrating on cookery and on recipes—had not been particularly appealing to the housewife.

Similarly, Avon cosmetics have over the last few years obtained a leading share in the U.K. cosmetic market through their own door-to-door demonstration approach, but again they needed to have high product quality in order to be successful.

Price can obviously be an important factor, depending on the value for money which the consumer believes that he is receiving from a particular product. Thus, in addition to Rolls Washing Machines and Books for Pleasure, Embassy have had a staggering success in the cigarette field by offering to the public not only a cigarette, but also a feeling that they were being thrifty in collecting the coupons. The effect was a func-tion of value which a price advantage could not have possibly achieved by itself.

At the same time, the value of an above average price in a new product launch is too often ignored. If there is an impor-tant enough market segment for the higher-priced product, or if the product category is an important purchase for the con-sumer, so that he or she may actually prefer to pay more for the reassurance of having bought high quality products, then the high price can be a positive benefit. Turtle Wax Car Polish, Horizon Holidays and many products in the fields of cosmetics, cars, gifts and products for babies are good examples. Similarly the Pergamon Press, probably the other most successful new venture in publishing in addition to Books for Pleasure since the war, concentrates on specialist books and periodicals at high prices. These high prices may be justified by the small runs but at the same time they must lend greater authority to the published material in the eyes of its specialist readership.

Opportunities for new product successes are greater either in undeveloped markets or in markets where the competition is still production-oriented. Thus Pickerings Pie Fillings found success in a new market, while Pergamon and Books for Pleasure were successful in a traditional one. G. B. Britton, are another good example of a relatively small company which has had great success in the traditional shoe market by realizing the need for branding. Aided by the new production processes which allowed it to offer a guarantee to the consumer, Britton launched first Tuf for men and then Gluv for women and have carved out for themselves a place in a market controlled hitherto by the retail outlets rather than by the brands themselves.

It is widely believed that it is the large companies which succeed in launching new products. For example, in his article in the *Financial Times* [1] W. Ramsay concluded from his analysis of grocery products that success in new product development is correlated with the size of the company concerned. This may be true of some markets but is certainly not true generally.

Thus only a large company could have developed Birds Eye Frozen Foods. Only a large company could have launched Camay in the very competitive soap market. Only a large company could have launched such a major cigarette brand as Embassy. Only a large company can launch a new car as Ford launched the Cortina.

On the other hand the successes of relatively small companies are remarkable. Wilkinson Sword, Pergamon Press,

1. 'Product Launches: The Facts', *Financial Times*, April 12, 1967.

Books for Pleasure, Pickerings Pie Fillings, Turtle Wax, Horizon Holidays, are obvious examples. And who would have thought a small company could almost overnight challenge and beat giants in the motor oil market such as Castrol, Shell and Esso? Duckhams have done just that.

It is clearly becoming more difficult for the small company to launch new products in highly competitive markets and even if the small company succeeds it is likely to be eventually absorbed in a large group. The resources and the organization of a large company can, however, also represent a disadvantage, as it is necessarily slow-moving and its executives do not have the entrepreneurial incentives of the small man. I am convinced that in the majority of fields there is still a great opportunity for the small company to launch successful new products.

four organization for development

importance of right organization

Although most consumer goods companies are convinced of the importance of innovation, there are great differences in the performance of the companies and these can be largely attributed to two factors which are closely related to each other:

1 attitude towards development.
2 organization for development.

There is a definite relation between the two factors because, although so many Company Boards talk of innovation, diversification, etc., as vital to their future, not many think this through to ensure that there is an appropriate organization within the company to evaluate opportunities and to take advantage of the most suitable ones. Yet it is noteworthy that organization is probably the most important single element in innovation and diversification. Booz, Allen and Hamilton mention that, when they conducted a survey about development problems among U.S. companies which had been relatirely successful with new products, the answers were as follows:

	% of companies reporting problem	% of problems reported
Organization	81	55
Control and follow up	35	12
Definition of objectives	26	9
Business analysis	26	9
New ideas and creativity	19	8
Personnel qualifications	14	5
Performance of steps	7	2

Eight companies out of ten mentioned organization as a problem and over half the problems concerned organization —four and a half times as many as those of the next most important factor.

different types of organization

Companies adopt different types of organization and there is no one type which is superior to the others in all cases. A company needs to experiment until it has found the most suitable development organization for its needs. The most frequent types are as follows:

1 R. and D. and top management.
2 Brand management.
3 Development committee.
4 Specialist development department.

1. R AND D AND TOP MANAGEMENT

Historically innovation took place on the initiative of the production side in a company which normally had the technical Research and Development role. When a technical advance was found, it was communicated to company management and a decision was quickly taken on whether to go ahead or not.

This procedure is much rarer now that we have discovered marketing orientation, but it still takes place in the small company which cannot afford a specialist marketing department and where the day-to-day commercial role is played by top management alone, often by the chief executive. This method has obviously all the virtues of fast communication translating itself into quick and flexible action—one of the main assets of a small company. It cannot, however, provide the thorough planning and evaluation which can be undertaken by other types of organization within a larger company.

2. BRAND MANAGEMENT

The larger companies have mainly adopted the brand management structure for their marketing needs, whereby marketing executives are assigned one brand or a group of brands for which they are responsible to marketing management. Many of these companies have assigned the marketing responsibility for new products to these brand managers. Either each brand manager is asked to develop new products connected with his range of products or one or more of them have responsibility for some current business as well as for all new products.

Such an arrangement has the important advantage that the person developing new products is well aware of the day-to-day position on the company's current products and so there should be few problems in relating the new product programme to that of the current operation. There should also be no difficulties in deciding whether current or new products demand higher technical development priority.

Nevertheless, I am convinced that generally it is a very bad system to have brand managers responsible for new products. My reasons are as follows:

1 Running brands have always problems demanding urgent attention and it is a brave man who decides to take his mind away from a product currently generating profit (or loss!) in order to think of a hypothetical profit and loss forecast possibly seven years hence. Naturally this executive is normally judged on the performance of the current products for which he is responsible, so more often than not the new product side is understandably neglected.

2 If several brand managers look after development projects related to their products, the result is that line extensions may be developed, but no one is looking out for suitable opportunities which may exist outside the company's existing product fields.

3 The qualities of a good brand manager may not necessarily be those of a good new product developer. The latter needs to combine with a strong practical streak

analytical aptitudes enabling him to take a cold objective look at the company's future and at the whole range of possible opportunities open to it, in order to select the most suitable ones. This combination is hardly the best one for the executive maximizing the day-to-day profit of a product.

The reasons mentioned above and particularly the first one mean that, in practice, I have found that such an organization leads to very little development action. I have even come across a well documented case of a company which for various reasons changed its development organization five times in about five years. After having had brand managers dealing with development, it created a new product development department. It then went back to the old system, after some time recreated the development department, then reverted to brand management and finally settled once more on the specialist department. The correlation between the type of organization and the level of development activity was most noticeable. To put it bluntly, every time brand management was responsible for development, nothing happened; every time there was a new product development department a great deal of activity was generated.

3. DEVELOPMENT COMMITTEE

A development committee often precedes the setting up of a specialist department and sometimes remains even after a department has been established.

Such a committee, normally consisting of the department heads concerned with development, e.g. marketing, sales, finance, R and D, can perform a useful function as a senior Board advising management on development. It also ensures that there is complete understanding of development policy and implementation among the relevant departments.

It is an illusion, however, to believe that such a committee can be a substitute for all the work which an individual needs to do to find and take advantage of an opportunity. The committee can guide and evaluate, but no more.

4. SPECIALIST DEVELOPMENT DEPARTMENT

Many of the larger and more efficient companies now have specialist development departments and it is obvious, in my opinion, that this represents the best type of organization for development, so long as the size of the company justifies it.
Only such a department, removed from the day-to-day worries and responsibilities of the current business, can formulate a detailed development policy for the company and implement it by means of a programme which may include both new product development and acquisitions. Not being restricted by too narrow a view of the business as it currently stands, the department has the scope of thinking in terms of the total field of operation open to the company.

There is, however, a danger that such a department may become classified as 'the backroom egg-heads' of the company, impractical academics who think of weird technological breakthroughs and produce tons of paper in report form, but are not really attuned to the mundane need for making profit.

It is fatal if such a situation is allowed to develop and so it is absolutely vital that the new product department should act not in isolation but in constant consultation with the other sides of the company, to ensure that there is full agreement with the development programme. After all the technical, marketing and sales departments will need to implement the thinking of the 'developers', so the latter must have the ability of enthusing the others that it will be in their interest to produce and market the new products.

It almost goes without saying that the development department must know fully what happens on current brands' marketing as well as on the R and D side, to ensure the suitability of the development programme. Yet, as an outside consultant, I have introduced more than once the new product development manager to the chemist working on his projects!

new product development and management

The importance of a positive attitude towards development among a company's management has already been touched on. It is important to emphasize this point, however, because a company may have an excellent organization for development or excellent new product opportunities, yet it is bound to fail in launching new products without the necessary management support.

This may sound obvious, but in fact many opportunities and considerable effort are often wasted in companies. Elaborate projects are worked out—often lasting a number of years —expenditure takes place on technical development and on market research only for management to delay taking a decision on launching in an area or nationally. Such delays need not be due to doubt that the project is a good one. Fear of risk or, to put it bluntly, cowardice is an important element in the delay. At the last minute the Board begin to question whether new products are a good thing. It is so much easier and safer to do nothing and hope that profits from existing products are maintained and so the file on the new product launch goes into the proverbial drawer.

It is wrong to criticize such reactions unduly as prudence is essential in development and undue enthusiasm has led to so many failures. What is to be criticized, however, is the fact that so much development work and expenditure have been allowed to take place if the management are not suitably motivated.

It is important, therefore, for the management to have an attitude towards development which is related to the development activity within the company. Either the Board should be prepared to back suitable projects which meet defined criteria or it should not allow development activity to take place which will not be acted on.

It follows that in companies where management wants new products it must actively support the development activity through the many trials and tribulations normally associated with each project. Such active support can make a considerable difference to the progress of a new product.

Evidence of management support is shown by the responsibility given to the executives in charge of development. Whatever the organization, it is important that there should be a direct line to management in order to obtain the necessary support and liaison. This means, therefore, that a senior executive should be in charge of development to have the necessary contact with top management and also to have the authority to push the projects through all the relevant departments in the company. It is not easy to obtain the co-operation of the various departments for a new product when they are normally fully stretched on the important existing products. Therefore, unless an enthusiastic senior executive is there to ensure that the new products are given their due attention, it is too easy for the projects to grind to a halt.

new product development and other departments

Liaison with management and the importance of management support have already been stressed. But this is not enough. It is obvious that development as a function relies on many company departments, but this is not obvious enough to prevent an ivory tower situation in some companies. Yet the developer, if he is to be successful, needs to become the focal point for his activity within the company.

Whatever the detailed organization for development, the normal company organization looks something like that shown overleaf.

The closest possible relationship must exist with the market research and R and D specialists who will help with the development process as well as with the production, marketing and sales executives who will inherit it at a later stage. Yet, despite this, everyone must be fully involved even at the beginning. I know of instances where the developers worked for years in perfecting a project until they finally unveiled it to the marketing and sales department with the attitude

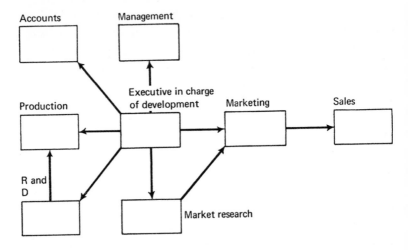

'Here it is. Is it not marvellous? Take it from here'. It is not surprising that projects are poorly received in such circumstances and that all possible faults are found. It is vital that the marketing, sales and production executives, to whom the responsibility will eventually pass, should have the chance of contributing at a very early stage. They would find it more difficult to criticize later!

Similarly the closer the contact between development, R and D and market research, the better the results. Ideally R and D should be in the development department rather than being responsible to the production director as usually happens for historical reasons. It is not enough to give R and D a brief and wait for the answer, because in practice development represents a constant series of compromises and formulation changes which can be angled towards consumer requirements, if there is a close team operation between the marketing and the technical specialists.

the attributes of a good development executive

The qualities necessary for the post of a new product development man make him sound a superman. He should have a strong personality capable of generating enthusiasm and of persuading to his point of view both management and other departments. He should be tactful to make others believe when necessary that the project is their idea rather than his. He should be creative, possessing enough imagination to look at the future and foresee opportunities. Yet he must also be analytical, weighing up the risks of each project and the odds of success. Finally, I believe he needs to have a strong pragmatic streak, to ensure that he never puts technique above result. There is a strong temptation to be carried away by the interest of the work into sociology, economics, crystal gazing, etc. Yet the sole purpose of the exercise is to make money through development and no developer should forget this. It follows therefore that a bent for figures is important if financial considerations are to be given their due importance.

In practice, of course, no one person has all the necessary attributes and one needs to compromise as best one can. Once the person has become a developer, it is often found that the post serves as an excellent training ground for it represents possibly one of the most challenging areas in a company and exposes the individual to detailed financial knowledge of the company's operation.

Thus companies may assign to the senior executive in charge of development assistants who, after a spell in development, often move on to other roles within the company. It has been found particularly useful to put such a junior executive in charge of the day-to-day progress of a new product, being responsible to the senior development manager. If the project surmounts the various hurdles and reaches the launching stage when the marketing department or the executives in charge of running brands take over, the junior development executive could well go over to the 'running product' side, to look after the project which he had nursed from the beginning. His knowledge of the project, his experience and usually his enthusiasm often make him into a valuable brand manager and the continuity of the project from development to marketing as a going brand is assured.

the role of an outside consultant

A company should consider the possibility of using an outside consultant, in addition to its organization, in order to deal with its new product development. Consultants could contribute wide experience in many markets which would probably be far wider than that of the company's executives. Their main contribution, however, would be in providing objective advice, being the only party without any financial interest in the success or failure of a new product.

The problem of preserving objectivity can be particularly acute in connection with new products. Executives within the company are often subjected to severe personal and political pressures, as has already been mentioned, so that the decision whether to proceed with a new idea or not could depend more on who thought of it rather than on its worth.

Moreover new ideas have a way of generating a life of their own within the company. A market study is done, possibly followed by some research. Some technical development takes place. Long term profit and loss forecasts are prepared showing what are, in writing, splendid figures at the end of perhaps year six or seven. It is not surprising, therefore, that in such circumstances the project is received with constantly greater enthusiasm.

If the project is good, then the enthusiasm is appropriate. If, however, it turns out to look unprofitable for the company, it is in practice extremely difficult for the company to reverse its previous enthusiasm. Every conceivable extenuating argument is sought to explain why the project is better than it looks and so why it should proceed to the next stage. It is tempting to remember the mythical profit figures allocated to the product at the end of the line and so to force the project through to national launch, whatever the indications regarding its failure or success.

Similarly the advertising agency—the only other organization normally involved in the launch of a new product—will have an important incentive to advise that the project should be progressed as the advertising appropriation spent on the launch would obviously profit the agency. It is improbable that this factor would directly influence an agency with a long term relationship with the company, but it is likely that, almost unconsciously, the agency will be inclined towards a recommendation to proceed with the project.

In the circumstances, when both the company and the agency have an interest in proceeding, it is not surprising that there have been so many disastrous new product launches and often one could have predicted the disaster. The most experienced and sophisticated companies have undergone such disasters and failure in retaining objectivity is the one main reason which I have already advanced for their occurrence.

The role of the consultant is clear, therefore. He can be useful in redressing the balance of attitudes towards the project by counselling caution and asking: 'What are the odds on the project succeeding?' At the same time, a consultant is no substitute for the right company organization and attitude regarding development. He can only advise, while the responsibility for the development policy and its implementation lies very clearly with the company.

five Where is the company going?

It is clear that development and diversification in some companies follow a detailed long-term strategy providing guidance on where the company is going. In other companies, on the other hand, there does not seem to be an operating development policy and decisions are taken on an opportunist *ad hoc* basis.

attitudes against planning

All too often company managements do not think that it is important to ask themselves where the company is going or, if they do ask, they do not strive hard enough to find the answer and to follow the policy thus fashioned.

The general lack of long range planning is not really surprising for various reasons. The main ones seem to be as follows:

1. FORECASTS ARE WRONG ANYWAY

Even short-term forecasts are often wrong. Medium and long term ones can be disastrous. The National Plan, for example, prepared with great care in the U.K., had to be jettisoned, after only a few months.

In the circumstances, why should a company indulge in planning in order to arrive at misleading conclusions which could prove positively dangerous?

2. WE HAVE DONE WELL WITHOUT PLANNING

Companies have been most successful till now without formalized planning, often through the entrepreneurial gifts of one man at the top. Changing over to planning procedures is not only expensive but could have a stultifying effect on a company operating flexibly and dynamically according to the needs of the moment.

3. PLANNING IS EXPENSIVE

Long-range planning requires expensive specialists who in turn require considerable budgets to justify their existence. If one bears in mind the inaccuracies of planning and the apparent lack of need for it, costs appear inordinately high.

Arguments such as those mentioned above are strong ones and are often used in justification for the lack of planning. Yet possibly the underlying reason is a very simple one—companies live for today only and are afraid of planning which may lead to some sacrifice of the short-term in return for long-term benefits. And this attitude is by no means limited to small companies only. Let me give four examples:

1 Company 'A' was run after the war as a U.K. subsidiary of a very large U.S. company by a man who was partly remunerated on a commission basis. Being near retirement age, he was clearly not interested in building for the long-term if this meant sacrificing current profits and it was notable that the company lost several opportunities by not backing new products with marketing support which was justified by long-term considerations.

2 Company 'B' is one of the most important international food companies, yet attention is paid to the current year's sales—even ex-factory rather than consumer—without relating the present to the future. Decisions are thus necessarily short-sighted and at times even harmful for the long-term.

3 Company 'C' is again an international company which has had a number of chairmen in recent years. All have made impressive promises to shareholders and long-term poli-

cies have had to be abandoned in order to meet the short-term promises.

4 Company 'D' is an international company which sells what it produces instead of adopting a marketing approach. Its policy is therefore necessarily short-term and it does not recognize the principle of long-term investment which is crucial, of course, to long-range planning.

the need to plan

Despite the arguments already advanced against planning and its absence in many companies, this situation cannot continue. In order to survive companies will need to take planning seriously if they are not already doing so.

After all, it was relatively easy for companies to survive in the sellers' markets which existed in most countries after the last war. The balance has since changed and most companies everywhere will agree that they are facing fiercer competition than ever before. Planning must be an important aspect of facing competition. There are important additional factors which make planning so important. The main ones are as follows:

1. CHANGES IN CONSUMER PATTERNS

Certain trends can be seen which suggest that the consumer and his habits will change fairly radically within, say, the next twenty years. For example, as a country becomes more prosperous, its expenditure on food falls in relation to total consumer expenditure and there is a trend towards high protein products and against carbohydrates. Thus consumption of products such as bread and potatoes falls, while meat consumption increases correspondingly.

Sociologically there are likely to be changes, tending towards the spread of a middle-class society on the Scandinavian pattern. Age patterns could well be different. For example, in the U.K. it is forecast that there will be a preponderance of very young and very old people whereas there will be a relative shortage of persons in the intervening age groups. Geographically there could be vital changes—again in the U.K. it looks as though, unless Government policy causes a complete reversal of current trends, the population will continue to move to the Midlands and to the South East.

Such considerations are clearly crucial to the future of a company.

2. CHANGES IN SIZE OF COMPANIES

Some forecasts have been made recently which suggest that in the foreseeable future a small number of companies will dominate consumer markets. For example, H. Dougier[1] has suggested that by 1985 the total world market will be more than double its present size and that in some thirty years' time up to 75 per cent of the world's business will be conducted by no more than 200–300 huge corporations, all completely international and organized accordingly.

However vague such a forecast may be, there has been a clear trend in this direction in many countries and the indications are that in an advanced economy a stage is reached when a few companies achieve domination in consumer goods. If this is accepted a company has a few clear cut alternatives:

1 go out of business.
2 aim to be part of a major group.
3 be small and flexible enough to cater for minority markets which would not be interesting to large groups.
4 obtain an important franchise which will stand up to competition from a large group, e.g. by controlling its own outlets.

What a company cannot afford to do is to take no decision to cater for such a situation. And detailed planning will obviously be necessary to make a reasonable decision.

1. *European Business* (France), H. Dougier, January 1968.

3. NEED FOR NEW PRODUCTS

The need to develop new products or diversify has been clearly established if a company wants at least to retain its profits. It is certainly possible to buy companies or launch new products without planning, but the wrong decisions could well be taken unless there are clear goals to be reached. This is terribly obvious but is not done in practice. Yet surely a company needs to decide whether it is to remain in food or in consumer goods or whether any market is of interest so long as the financial returns are adequate. Only then can one decide whether a development is good or bad according to the agreed policy.

And if there are no clearly defined financial goals, which can only be set up within a proper planning framework, how can any project be judged to be good, bad or indifferent? There is no such thing as a good or a bad project in a vacuum. It is only good or bad in relation to a company's capabilities and aims. Need I repeat the need for planning?

4. MORE SOPHISTICATED PLANNING

It is very difficult to forecast technological innovations, but the continuing development of the computer will certainly help the planner in providing the required data and in increasing the accuracy of the forecasting. The more sophisticated techniques which should follow will provide a strong argument against the suspicions directed towards planning, even though it can never be expected that it can become an exact science.

how to plan

The most important thing is for a company's management to decide to plan. This is not enough, however. It must also decide to put the planning into practice. Just to adopt planning procedures because it is 'fashionable' or because the competition are doing it is, of course, a pointless exercise as decisions are then taken which do not take the planning into consideration.

It is particularly important that the management give a lead on these matters or at any rate that they fully accept the implications. There are companies where executives at a lower level are trying desperately to evolve long-term plans for the company without adequate support from the Board. This again is a useless exercise, as the management decisions are taken in complete separation from the planning.

Once the management accept planning and put it into operation, the method of planning will evolve naturally to fit the particular company's needs. One approach useful in laying a framework for planning is as follows:

1 Analysis of company's strengths and weaknesses.
2 Definition of financial criteria.
3 Estimates of future turnover and profits from existing products.
4 Definition of company's field of interest in the long-term.

Such a framework can best be illustrated with a mythical example.

1. ANALYSIS OF STRENGTHS AND WEAKNESSES

STRENGTHS	WEAKNESSES
Marketing	
High grocery distribution set up to distribute short shelf-life products. Strong company names both with trade and with consumer. Success in marketing mass consumer goods in competitive markets. International franchise and information flow.	Little capacity in sales forces. Strong sales seasonality in summer. High costs of overheads compare badly with competition. No franchise or experience in catering outlets.
Management	
Ability and intention to invest in good opportunities. Determination to plan and implement plans. Efficient organization.	Slow to make decisions. Little recruitment from outside means no experience of markets or techniques not known by company already.

STRENGTHS	WEAKNESSES
Technical	
Knowledge of food technology. Experience in canning and glass. Little seasonality in production. Some opportunities for increasing capacity on present plant. Favourable attitudes to innovation according to marketing needs.	Lack of freezing and Accelerated Freeze Drying (A.F.D.) facilities. Little technical knowledge of fields outside present product range.

2. FINANCIAL CRITERIA

a Return on capital—10 per cent after tax on Discounted Cash Flow basis.

b Net profit to average not less than £60,000 per year for each new project in first five years, £150,000 per annum thereafter.

c Break even to occur not later than Year 3 after national launch on a running basis.

d Cumulative break-even to occur not later than Year 4.

e Total company profit is to increase at an average of 8 per cent p.a. for next fifteen years.

The above would be intended not as a strait jacket, but as guidelines. Clearly a company should accept that certain projects will be viable even if some of the criteria are not adhered to, but in these cases the existence of such criteria will ensure that the exceptions made will be conscious rather than unconscious ones. Thus a good reason for proceeding with a project which goes against one or more of the criteria would be if there were compensating advantages, e.g. cumulative break-even is unlikely to occur before Year 6, but the estimated return on capital is 25 per cent.

3. ESTIMATES OF CURRENT BUSINESS

The life cycle of a product consisting of introduction, growth, maturity, saturation and decline is well known and widely accepted as a theory. The trend can be shown as follows:

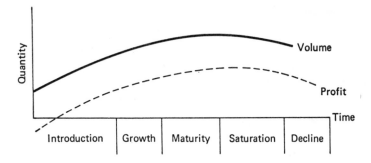

Obviously a brand can be revitalized and the volume and profit turned or certainly postponed. In general, however, a business cannot rely on long-term increases in profit by relying on current business alone and the following pattern could result:

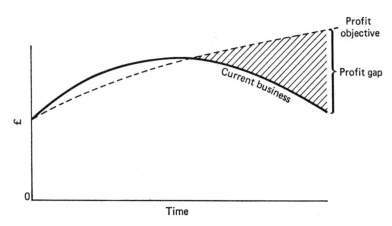

The shaded area shows the notorious profit gap — the difference between the profit objective and the estimated profit from current business

4. THE COMPANY'S FIELD OF INTEREST

This is, of course, crucial. In our mythical company's case it could be: 'Food products for the consumer, irrespective of what distribution channels are used.'

Such a policy would lead obviously to consideration for the future of outlets other than current ones, e.g. distribution of food products through garages. A direct approach to the public could also be examined, e.g. van selling on a door-to-door basis. Moreover, the whole food industry would be closely screened to isolate the right opportunities in markets not already covered by the company.

Yet the same company could take vastly different decisions which would alter the course of its progress. It could decide to stay in a narrow segment of the food market, possibly diversifying into catering. Or it could stay in grocery outlets only and expand into non-food grocery lines. Or it could take a wider view, by deciding to be in consumer goods handled through retail outlets, diversifying possibly into toiletries, cosmetics, pharmaceuticals, etc. Finally it could decide that it does not matter what field it is in, so long as the financial requirements are met, so a very wide vista would be open to it for scrutiny.

Such a decision where to go is difficult to take but needs to be taken on the basis of the analysis of the company's strengths and weaknesses, its financial aims and the 'profit gap'. Once it is made in conjunction with the other criteria, the company begins to know where it is going. A framework for development has been set and projects can be evaluated against set criteria. We are away!

six planning for the 1980's

long-range planning for consumer goods

Once the company has established its development policy, it needs to plan for both the short- and the long-term, in order to implement the policy.

It can be argued that the sequence is wrong, i.e. that it is impossible to determine the policy until the long-range planning and particularly the long-range forecasting have been completed. There is some truth in this argument and the company policy should certainly be reviewed and revised if necessary following the completion of the long-range planning. In practice, however, it is important for a policy to be determined at the beginning to limit and to direct the planning. Otherwise, if no restrictions are put on it, the planning would probably become unwieldy and would certainly take too long for a company to wait.

The reader may be surprised that consumer goods companies should plan so far ahead. After all, they do not require the development time or investment levels common in capital goods and the life cycle of consumer goods is becoming shorter and shorter. So what is the point of long-range planning in consumer goods?

U.K. consumer goods companies have certainly been slow to recognize the values of long-range planning as shown by a study conducted recently by Basil Denning of the London Graduate School of Business which was discussed at a conference on long-range planning in 1967.[1] Out of the 21 com-

1. *Long Range Planning — The Concept and the Need*, H. F. R. Perrin, National Conference on Long Range Planning, University of Bradford, November 1967.

panies in consumer distribution which had been approached, not one said that it had a planning system.

This attitude is changing, however. 1967 saw an important growth of interest in long-range planning in general in the U.K., and the newly formed Long-Range Planning Society had 500 members in the first six months, many of them from consumer goods companies.

Even if long-range planning must be essential to capital goods industries in particular, its usefulness in consumer goods is clear for the following reasons:

1 Many consumer goods industries, e.g. consumer durables, have a long time lag between planning and the final implementation.

2 The actual processes and attitudes involved in long-range planning have considerable benefit in giving the company's executives a new sense of perspective.

3 Even if the life-cycle of individual products is very short— and there is still insufficient evidence on this vital point apart from the Nielsen study on packaged goods only—the investment necessary to enter a market tends to be increasing, so it is extremely important to ensure that the direction in which the company is heading is appropriate.

For example, a recent study of a food market up to 1980 indicated that certain sections of it would be far more important than they are now and, in the light of this forecast, the company concerned embarked immediately on a development programme in the relevant area. Even if the new products come to the end of their life-cycle by, say, 1975, the company will be in a good position to build up its franchise in this section by launching more new products and so will have anticipated the long-term opportunity.

4 The various environmental changes which we are undergoing—political, technological, economic, sociological, demo-

graphic and other changes—and which will continue to affect us, probably to an increasing degree, influence consumer markets considerably and long-term forecasting in these areas needs to be taken into account for consumer goods almost as much as for capital goods. For example, those consumer goods companies which have laid long-established plans for the time when the U.K. enters the Common Market are likely to benefit at the expense of the companies which hardly consider the implications until the entry into some kind of European community is announced, as would seem most likely.

use of historical data

A look at the future must obviously start with a study of the past. It is a cliché that available statistics are not used adequately and this is certainly true in relation to long-range planning. A company normally analyses adequately such data as market shares, distribution, breakdowns by outlet, area, class, age, etc.

Yet this is mechanical information consisting of what everyone knows should always be included in a market appraisal. The development executive needs very much more information such as:

1 BRAND LOYALTY Is it easy or difficult to persuade the user of one brand to try another?

2 SATISFACTION The extent of satisfaction with existing products. Are there defects in current products and would consumers be interested in products with different attributes?

3 ATTITUDES TO COST/QUALITY/CONVENIENCE How important is the product to the consumer and would the latter be prepared to pay more for a higher degree of quality or of convenience? For example, before launching the techmatic razor in the U.K., Gillette would have needed to know how much more they could charge in comparison with their normal shaving products.

4 PAST NEW PRODUCT HISTORY What happened when new products were launched in this market in the past? If they failed, why did they fail? Could the failures be attributed to the individual product or to the company or to the market in general?

5 THE COMPETITION What kind of companies are there in the market? It is often possible to assess on the basis of their actions in this and in other markets how strong they are competitively and how they would react against an important new product.

6 MARKET REACTION TO CHANGES Has the market reacted strongly to important product packaging or marketing changes in the past or have the trends remained constant whatever the changes? Some markets have proved to be very susceptible to any change, whereas others have been extremely difficult to move from the existing pattern. The latter would normally be more difficult markets in which to make an impression, other things being equal.

7 RELATION TO ENVIRONMENTAL CHANGES Is there a correlation between economic, sociological and demographic changes and the consumption patterns in the market?

For example, car ownership must be affected by trends in urban development. Consumer durables in general show a close correlation with trends in disposable income and with credit facilities. Even among low-priced staple goods the effect of economic squeezes can be seen in certain instances.

To find out the importance of the correlation between the market and environmental changes on the basis of historical data is clearly a useful foundation for any long-range forecasting.

8 INTERNATIONAL DATA What are the trends in other countries? Is there any pattern which can be applied to the U.K.?

Use of international data is normally low and few companies realize how relatively cheap it is to obtain comparative data on broad market trends.

It is not enough to look at, say, the U.S.A. and assume that U.S. per capita consumption of a product if higher than that of the U.K.—it invariably is—represents the future U.K. potential. Such a comparison has been found misleading because of the many differences and because of the gulf in the standard of living between the two countries. If, however, comparative data for a number of countries are examined, say the U.S.A., Canada, Sweden, West Germany, France, U.K., it is at times possible to find the correlation between a certain level of consumption and a certain standard of living. This can then be applied to future U.K. forecasts in the light of various assumptions regarding the future trends in the U.K. economy.

sociological and demographic forecasting

A number of trends can be clearly seen for the future, many of them being the continuation of recent changes. According to Maurice Zinkin,[1] the two most important trends in the U.K. will be the disappearance of poverty and the changing importance of women in our society.

Both these trends are very likely to continue and to lead to a number of allied changes affecting many markets. For example, it seems reasonable to suppose that we will develop into a classless type of society similar to that in Scandinavia and that the current habits of the ABC1 classes and of London and the South East will spread in time to the rest of the U.K. In this context, it is noteworthy that the current food consumption pattern in London and the South of England is closer to Sweden than to the rest of the U.K. in its bias towards protein and away from carbohydrate foods. The increase in working wives is bound to lead to a corresponding increase in consumer discretionary income and to even greater stress

1. Paper to Advertising Association Conference, M. Zinkin, May 1966.

than before on high-priced convenience items. The extra disposable income is likely to lead to much greater ownership of cars and other durables which in turn will have important implications on other markets, e.g. transportation, holidays, frozen foods, etc.

Automation and a richer society will lead to an increase in leisure and leisure activities. At the same time this is likely to be accompanied by a trend towards anxiety and mental stress if Swedish evidence is relevant.

Whatever the political future is likely to hold, whether we join or do not join the Common Market, through foreign travel and through the growth of international media we will become more Europeanized than before. The differences between us and the Continent will be less marked than the similarities.

The age distribution of the U.K. population will probably change radically, as has already been mentioned. The relative increase in the importance of the youngest and of the oldest age groups will certainly lead to greater potential for baby and for geriatric products.

Retail distribution is an area which could well see great changes by 1980. Apart from even greater concentration into a few hands, it is possible that there will soon exist methods of shopping by computer from the home, as described very vividly in a recent issue of the *Harvard Business Review*.[1] This system is already technically feasible in the U.S.A. and seems to present greater convenience to the consumer, particularly to the working housewife.

At the same time, there will be counter trends as sections of the public combat the main trends in an effort to impose their individuality. For example, it is interesting that in North America most wallpaper is self-adhesive, but, if one wants to be 'different', one can buy the premium type of wallpaper which needs paste.

Thus, although there will be general trends towards con-

1. 'Next Revolution in Retailing', A. F. Doody and W. R. Davidson, *Harvard Business Review*, May/June 1967.

venience products, it is likely that the consumer will seek to compensate by using products and services which specifically demand labour. It is possible in this context to visualize the working housewife using ready-made food during the week, but making elaborate meals, perhaps baking her own cakes and even her bread during the weekend. Similarly growth of a retail service based on computers and on buttons which the housewife can operate at home could well be accompanied by a resurgence of the small counter service family shop to serve her individual needs.

Altogether it is certain that there will be very much more market segmentation than there is now, as has already happened in the United States. More and more consumers will try to assert their individualism by using products which they will feel are not used by the masses and so are 'exclusive' to them.

The possibilities mentioned above are but a few of the factors which should be examined and on whose future trends assumptions would need to be made, according to the particular project.

If the events during the period 1953–68 are analysed, it can be seen how important are the changes which have taken place during this period and how they have affected various markets, e.g. cars, bicycles, mail order, appliances, etc. The next few years are certain to be at least as eventful and a well informed guess needs to be made at what will happen then, in order to assess the implications for companies operating in the U.K.

economic forecasting

If the analysis of historical data has shown that there is a relationship between economic trends and changes in the markets in which the company is interested, it is well worth while to forecast these economic trends for the future.

It is true that this is no easy task and the fate of the U.K. National Plan shows the hazards of economic forecasting. It is easier, however, to forecast for the longer term as unexpected short-term events such as an economic squeeze, a change in taxation or in H.P. terms and even devaluation are all events which may have great importance over markets at a particular time, but are relatively less important when seen in the perspective of a fifteen- or twenty-year plan.

It seems, therefore, reasonable to make certain long-term assumptions for the U.K. economy, e.g. that we will eventually cure our present economic *malaise* and that G.N.P. will be able to maintain an annual rate of growth of 3–4 per cent for a large number of years.

Against the level of G.N.P. one can set certain levels of disposable consumer income and consumer markets will be considered as a proportion of that income, on the basis of past data and of assumptions on future trends of total disposable income.

Use of international data, particularly of more advanced economics, can also point to certain future trends, as already mentioned. If study of historical international data has shown that there is a broad correlation between certain consumption levels and a certain 'standard of living'—and many such correlations have been found—then this factor can be considered in relation to the U.K. market when the latter is forecast to reach that 'standard of living'.

Although the process of economic forecasting may sound vague, being based on arguable assumptions and fraught with many problems of definition, it has been found in fact to be most useful in conjunction with the other types of forecasting to point to future market sizes, trends and patterns. Forecasts of the effects of trends in one market on other markets can be particularly useful and in this connection it would be important to develop input/output analysis. At the moment, I believe that input/output is very difficult to use for economic forecasting because the tables take a long time to produce and are so often out of date, while the categories separately are too broad and often one category includes many large markets with completely different trends. I believe, however, that, as industry begins to recognize the usefulness of input/output analysis and as computer systems are developed further, this will become an important tool in economic forecasting.

technological forecasting

However good economic, sociological and demographic forecasting may be, it could easily be confounded by important technological breakthroughs. For example, all trends in medical products and in food would have to be turned upside down following the discovery of antibiotics and of frozen foods respectively.

Until recently haphazard technological developments have dictated the direction and the speed of change. Now, however, various techniques are being used to foresee the possibility of these technological developments and so to try to influence them. According to Erich Jantsch,[1] about 600 large and medium U.S. companies currently conduct technological forecasting on a regular basis. For example, the Xerox Corporation is aiming for a turnover of $2,000m. in 1975 and half of it is supposed to be represented by innovation based on technological forecasting.

Outside the United States there is probably little technological forecasting on a systematic basis, but this is likely to change very shortly as companies become aware of its usefulness. The expansion of the Stanford Research Institute into Europe, following its remarkable success in selling its forecasting services in the U.S. since it started in 1958, is an important pointer.

It would be wrong to claim too much for technological forecasting. Chance will always play an important part in technological breakthroughs and the timing of such developments will be extremely difficult to estimate. Nevertheless the work done so far clearly shows the usefulness of the technique, even at this early stage in its development. Although R and D experts will claim with some justification that they have prac-

1. 'Forecasting the Future', *Science Journal*, October 1967.

tised it for many years, technological forecasting should provide a disciplined method of obtaining the following information:

1 a rough indication of possible technological developments within a broad time scale.
2 the probability that the above developments can be achieved.

If a company has the above information, it is then in a position to direct its resources to anticipate the breakthroughs and even to influence them. We have already seen on a national scale how the recent American and Russian concentration of resources on the space programme has led to developments in this area which have been very much greater than in most other fields. Similarly, if on a more modest scale, it seems possible for a company to concentrate its resources in a field where there appears to be good opportunity for a breakthrough, so long as there is an important commercial opportunity.

The main techniques for technological forecasting can be broadly described as follows:

1 THE DELPHI MODEL Developed by the Rand Corporation in the United States, this technique basically consists of a series of interviews with experts expected to be in a position to have a view on future technological developments.

For example the experts could first be asked by means of individual interviews what breakthroughs they expect in, say, the next thirty years. When the answers are analysed and the most popular breakthroughs listed, the same experts would be asked about the probability of achieving these breakthroughs over the time span of thirty years. The study could then be refined further by narrowing down on the time scale of the most popular and most probable breakthroughs.

2 EXTRAPOLATING TRENDS Study of past developments in a particular industry can lead to useful extrapolation of future trends so long as an attempt is made to quantify the advance necessary at each stage.

3 NORMATIVE FORECASTING Whereas the above two approaches start from the present, normative forecasting starts from a future goal and works back. Thus one could start with a likely development such as mass travel to the moon and then consider the implications and the steps which will need to be taken before this can become reality.

Many other techniques have been developed. The O.E.C.D. survey on the subject[1] listed 20 basic approaches and 100 different variations. These are not as important, however, as the broad principle. Once a company has accepted the importance of technological forecasting, it should not be difficult to devise the most suitable approach for its individual needs.

In many cases companies without the necessary resources to develop and back important technological developments may think that technological forecasting is not for them. In fact even a company with the necessary resources could decide that the most profitable policy is to be second in a new field rather than first, as George Cyriax recently argued.[2]

Ansoff and Stewart[3] believe that a company interested in a field where technological change is important has four basic approaches it can take:

1 *Be the first* by pursuing a rigorous policy of technical innovation entailing both high risks and great opportunities.

2 *follow the innovator* by developing again strong R and D resources and an organization which would allow the

---

1. *Technological Forecasting in Perspective*, Erich Jantsch, O.E.C.D., Paris, 1967.
2. 'The Case for Being Second', George Cyriax, *Financial Times*, 3rd April 1968.
3. 'Strategies for technology based business', H. Ansoff and J. Stewart, *Harvard Business Review*, November/December 1967.

company to move extremely fast and copy the innovator, learning from the latter's mistakes.

3 *appeal to specific markets* by adapting the innovator's products to specific market requests.

4 *launch me-too products,* i.e. launch very similar products to those first marketed by the innovator, aiming to find if possible some kind of advantage in terms of cost or manufacturing method.

At first sight the first and possibly the second policies seem to be the most attractive for a company, but the others should certainly not be written off if only because of the long time normally necessary to develop a new product representing a real innovation. Adler [1] analysed recently the time lag in the development of 42 such products. According to his findings, the period of time elapsing between the birth of the idea and the subsequent launch amounted to 55 years for television, 30 for zip fasteners, 18 for minute rice, 15 for frozen foods, polaroid camera, penicillin and Xerox. At the same time Gerber baby foods took only one year and Johnson's liquid shoe polish only 3 years.

Thus the gestation period varies greatly depending on the industry and in many cases is extremely long, though the average length is certain to decrease as technology advances and as technological forecasting serves to focus companies' attention on a small number of technologies.

It is, therefore, important for the company to determine its attitude towards innovation and decide whether it intends to be the innovator, be the second in the market, appeal to specialist markets or launch me-too products. There is no general answer, as this will depend very much on the company concerned and on the markets in which it is interested.

Once the company has determined its policy on this point, it will be able to assess the importance of technological forecasting as far as its individual needs are concerned. I believe

1. 'Time lag in new product development', L. Adler, *Journal of Marketing*, January 1966.

that the technique will be useful in its broad aspects to every company if only for defensive reasons, but will be particularly important to the innovator and to the company which wants to be second.

practical applications of long-range planning

When the projections based on historical data are married to those arising from sociological, demographic, economic, technological and other relevant forecasts, the company has before it a picture of the future trends in its existing markets and in any other markets in which it is interested by definition.

At this stage there may well be a case for revising the company development policy if the long-range planning has changed the expected scope for the company in its existing markets or has uncovered important opportunities outside the defined interest of the company. There needs to be a certain amount of flexibility in both procedure and attitude if long-range planning is to be used to best effect.

It is clearly useful to look at the future, but only if, as a result, the company's operation is more profitable than it would have been otherwise. Long-range planning can and should play an important part in the development process, but it is only useful in its applications. This may sound obvious but too often in practice companies, if they have been persuaded to use it, have become enthusiastic with the technique itself rather than in the end product and it is not surprising that in the United States there has been recently much disenchantment with long-range planning.

David Ewing[1] estimated in his article that there were some 1,000 companies in the United States with planning departments and, where they did not exist, other executives devoted much of their time to planning. One of the main problems seems to be a human one, i.e. that the planners should not deal with the outside environment only, but should stand

1. 'Corporate Planning at a Crossroads', D. W. Ewing, *Harvard Business Review*, July/August 1967.

with feet firmly on the ground and consider the environment in relation to the company's resources. The rest of the company, on the other hand, should ensure that the planning, so long as it is practical, should be understood and translated into practical decisions. Otherwise, as Ewing says, there is a great danger that the planners will go one way and the managers and administrators another and the two sides will never meet.

It is vital, therefore, that a company regard long-range planning in the correct context and that there should be understanding of what it can and what it cannot do. One should not expect too much from such attempts at gazing into a crystal ball, however well informed and technical the gazing may be.

Long-term forecasting should be used as a directional technique to be constantly revised, guiding and directing the company, but not dictating the decisions. The estimates at any one point in time must be regarded as in the context of the long-term pattern and it would be disastrous to regard them as completely accurate.

It is also useless if the long-range planning function becomes viewed as an academic exercise—interesting and perhaps worthy of a paper in a professional journal, but completely pointless from the practical point of view. This is a situation which can well occur as long-range planning demands a high order of imagination and intellect from the individuals concerned.

Such an individual, when faced with the fascinating challenge of forecasting the future, can easily find himself carried away by the interest in the subject and will forget the company's limited needs.

It is important, therefore, to treat long-range planning in a strictly pragmatic way by considering at every stage the applications of the planning to company profitability. If such a 'materialistic' approach is adopted and if the company management recognize the importance of long-range planning, it will play a vital role in the company's development and diversification decisions. Some examples of its application in consumer goods' companies will serve to illustrate its usefulness.

1 Company A had made a major policy decision to enter into a long-term plant rebuilding programme. Detailed forecasts of the most likely trends in its markets over the following thirteen years, combined with an assessment of trends in the various market segments, enabled the company to make better decisions regarding future plant needs than they would have done on the basis of forecasts founded on past data alone. Moreover the company was able to take immediate decisions to concentrate on certain market segments in preparation for future trends.

2 Company B had a full short-term development programme, but analysis of its profit gap indicated need to have additional development projects to be consumer tested about five years later. A long-range planning study was conducted, therefore, to provide long-term forecasts for a large number of markets which enabled the company to select a short list of suitable markets for long-term diversification.

3 Company C had decided that, in the long term, its main strength was in the field of technological innovation. A long-range planning programme was devised, therefore, with the specific object of isolating suitable markets in which it was thought likely that completely new product concepts could be developed.

4 Long-range planning on a practical and even empirical basis has obviously played an important part in the growth of Batchelors Foods in the U.K.[1] Bought by Unilever in 1943, its business was concentrated very largely in canned peas and the company name was Batchelors Peas Limited.

This remained the situation in the early 1950's and it was clear that the opportunities to expand in canned peas were limited.

It was decided, therefore, to change the company name to

1. *Long Range Planning in Practice*, A. J. Goodall, National Conference on Long Range Planning, University of Bradford, November 1967.

Batchelors Foods Limited and to take advantage of Unilever financial, marketing and technical resources to extend into other food areas.

A diversification programme combining short- and long-term development took place and as a result the company has grown considerably in both turnover and profits, following the launch of such products as packet soups, Vesta meals, Surprise dehydrated vegetables and Promise pie-kits. The entry into packet soups was a quick decision based on U.S. experience. The other products followed considerably longer planning.

All the above examples show how long-range planning can be used in an intensely practical manner and in each case it is certain that very different decisions would have been taken if only current and past data had been analysed.

The Batchelors example is particularly useful as it illustrates the combination of short- and long-term action. The company cannot forget its profit position and wait for detailed and lengthy forecasts, so quick development such as that of Batchelors packet soups must follow quickly while the long-range planning is taking place.

It is also possible to uncover immediate opportunities in the midst of the long-range planning. If this happens, as it has happened to me a number of times, I would advocate quick action so long as the opportunity warrants it. And if this means that the long-range planning needs to be jettisoned for the moment, let it be. The long-range planning must be the servant and not the master of the company!

seven isolation of market opportunities

find the market for the company

When the company's development policy has been established, and if it has been decided to look for new markets, it follows that the next step must be to isolate the most suitable markets for the company, ideally in the context of long-range forecasting.

Although the process of market search sounds simple in theory, in practice it is not. After all there are so many companies in the hunt these days that, if there is an obvious market with great potential for new entrants, one can be assured that dozens of companies are considering it at the same time. Thus a number of companies entered the slimming product field in the early 1960's because it was thought that this market presented considerable growth. The large majority 'retired hurt' when the forecasts were proved to be wrong. Similarly, in consumer appliances most major companies have a dishwasher either ready or near completion, as has already been mentioned. Men's toiletries is another market into which many companies launched products simultaneously with high hopes and generally with poor results. Women's cosmetics is a field in which a multitude of companies are interested at the moment and doubtless many of these will suffer from this concentration of interest.

Moreover it has been proved again and again that there is no such thing as a good or a bad market opportunity. An opportunity is only good or bad for the particular company concerned and what may be excellent for one company could be completely unsuitable even for its nearest competitor and vice versa. The two examples below illustrate this point.

1 A consumer goods company had developed a product which, with some changes in formulation, could enter two completely different markets. The two alternatives were carefully assessed and financial forecasts were made for both.

It was clear that one opportunity was superior to the other on the basis of the assumptions made. At the same time the better opportunity was riskier than the other, demanding considerably larger marketing expenditures and it involved competition with strong marketing companies.

Such an approach was contrary to the company's experience and attitude, as it has been successful by always trying to be a large fish in a small pond and by avoiding strong competition. It would, therefore, be at a disadvantage in choosing a good but strongly competitive opportunity. Its management would be inexperienced in such a situation. The same would apply in the case of the sales force. The trade would be surprised by such a sudden change in policy. Even the consumer might notice.

It was decided, therefore, to choose the second opportunity which did not require such risks. It needed smaller expenditure and the market was not particularly competitive. It fitted closely with the company's strengths and weaknesses, even though it was recognized to be theoretically the inferior opportunity. And the results so far show the wisdom of the decision.

2 Another consumer goods company believed that its main skill lay in marketing and in meeting tough competition. If the market was really tough it did not matter so long as the opportunity was good enough. The company believed that it could beat most of the competition both in financial resources and in marketing skill.

A market was agreed, therefore, as suitable for diversification which would certainly have been unacceptable to the company in the previous example and would probably have been wrong for most companies without the same attitude and the same resources.

I trust, therefore, that the need to find suitable markets for the individual company has been established. This does not mean that a company must always stay in the same type of market and cannot change its attitudes. It is very much a matter of degree and timing. A company which for 50 years has relied on technological advantages and has not developed much in marketing skills should surely not go into a detergent-type of market without years of gradual and well planned preparation. Companies can change over time, however, Batchelors Foods being a good example of such a long-term transformation.

screening systems

Once the need is seen to find markets suitable to the company's current profile or to its future characteristics if important changes are planned, it follows that the company's strengths and weaknesses must be examined particularly closely in this context. Such an analysis combined with the development policy criteria should result in the definition of what factors are important in the search for new markets and in the relative importance of each individual factor.

Screening systems have been found useful for this purpose. They incorporate all the relevant factors and it is possible to weight the factors according to their importance.

An example of a screening system which has been used very successfully for some years is shown below:

1. Growth

  a Sterling Sales Trend

Weighting Factor

3

Declining market	−2
Static market	−1
Growth in line with population	0
Growth faster than population growth	+1
Growth much faster than population growth	+2

Weighting Factor

b Volume Trend   4

    Declining unit sales   −2
    Static unit sales   −1
    Growth in line with population   0
    Growth faster than population growth   +1
    Growth much faster than population growth   +2

c Long-term Prospects   6

    Almost certain decline   −2
    Probable decline   −1
    Likely static market   0
    Probable growth   +1
    Almost certain growth   +2

2. The Market

  a Current Market Size (R.S.P.)   3

    Under £2m.   −2
    £2m.–10m.   −1
    £11m.–20m.   0
    £20m.–40m.   +1
    £40m.+   +2

  b Buying by Class   1

    Strong C2DE bias   −2
    Some C2DE bias   −1
    Strong ABC1 bias   0
    General appeal   +1
    General appeal with some ABC1 bias   +2

  c Age Group Characteristics   2

    Concentration among old persons   −2
    Strong bias among older age groups   −1
    Little difference by age   0
    Some bias among young age groups   +1
    Strong bias among young age groups   +2

  d Area Profile   1

    Concentration in one or two areas   −2
    Strong regional differences   −1
    National appeal with Northern bias   0
    Uniform appeal nationally   +1
    National appeal with Southern bias   +2

3. Stability

  a Economic Factors   5

    Very sensitive to economic conditions   −2
    Fairly sensitive   −1
    Some sensitivity   0
    Should be reasonably stable   +1
    Strong continuous demand   +2

		Weighting Factor
b *Seasonality*		3

Sales concentrated in one month of the year	−2
Strong seasonality in one part of the year	−1
Two peaks during the year	0
Some seasonality	+1
No seasonality	+2

4. *Marketing Skills*

a *Penetration of Branding*		3

Dominated by two or three major brands	−2
One dominating brand with own brand element	−1
Fragmentation among many brands	0
Two or three brands with strong own brand element	+1
Commodity market moving towards branding	+2

b *Companies in the Market*		5

Three or more major marketing companies in market	−2
Market divided among two major marketing companies	−1
One major company in market	0
Market divided among two or three unsophisticated companies	+1
Market fragmented among a number of unsophisticated companies	+2

c *Marketing/Sales Ratio*		3

Very high expenditure	−2
High expenditure	−1
Average for consumer goods	0
Low expenditure	+1
Very low expenditure	+2

d *Product Differentation*		5

Little prospect of product advantage	−2
Uncertain prospect of product advantage	−1
Some prospects for slight advantages	0
Some prospects for important product advantages	+1
Good prospects for important product advantages	+2

5. *Image*

a *Company Image*		2

Weakens company image	−2
Inconsistent with image	−1
Makes no difference to image	0
Strengthens image	+1
Strengthens image very considerably	+2

Weighting Factor

b Brand Images

4

Cannot use company brand names	—2
Unlikely to use brand names	—1
Can possibly use brand names	0
Company brand names would be sensible	+1
Brand names would be positively helpful	+2

6. Production

a Technology

5

Very different technology unfamiliar to company required	—2
Fairly different technology unfamiliar to company	—1
Different technology but familiar to company	0
Similar technology	+1
Similar technology some capacity available	+2

b Buying Resources

3

Severe buying disadvantage compared with competition	—2
Some disadvantages	—1
No difference from competition	0
Competitive advantages	+1
Strong buying advantages	+2

7. Selling and Distribution

a Sales Force

6

Present sales force completely unsuitable	—2
Sales force compares badly with competition	—1
Equal to competition	0
Some competitive advantages	+1
Sales force capacity and strong competitive advantage	+ 2

b Distribution

5

Completely different outlets from those covered now	—2
Large extension needed to current distribution	—1
Some extension needed	0
Small extension needed	+1
Present distribution completely suitable	+2

Such a system, however crude, helps to ensure that all possible factors are taken into consideration and that every market is considered on a comparative basis. Each company should establish its own system and the scores and weighting factors will depend greatly on its characteristics.

If the above screen is applied to say eight markets, the following pattern could result.

Factor	Maximum Score	Market A	B	C	D	E	F	G	H
Sterling sales trend	6	6	0	−6	3	3	0	−3	0
Volume trend	8	4	−4	−8	0	4	0	−4	−4
Long-term prospects	12	0	0	−6	0	12	0	−6	0
Current market size	6	0	6	3	0	0	6	3	−3
Buying by class	2	1	1	1	−1	2	1	1	0
Age group characteristics	4	0	0	0	2	2	0	−2	0
Area profile	2	1	1	1	0	2	−1	0	1
Economic factors	10	5	5	0	−5	10	−5	5	0
Seasonality	6	−3	0	0	3	3	6	0	3
Penetration of branding	6	6	0	3	−6	3	0	3	0
Companies in the market	10	10	5	5	−10	5	5	5	5
Marketing/Sales ratio	6	3	0	0	−6	3	0	0	3
Product differentiation	10	5	0	5	0	5	0	−5	0
Company image	4	0	2	0	2	−2	2	0	4
Brand images	8	0	0	4	4	0	0	0	8
Technology	10	5	0	−5	−5	−5	0	0	5
Buying resources	6	0	3	0	−3	0	0	3	3
Sales force	12	6	0	6	−6	6	0	0	0
Distribution	10	5	0	5	0	−5	0	0	10
TOTAL	138	54	19	8	−28	48	14	0	35

The above table shows how a screening system can be used. On one sheet of paper eight markets are compared quantitatively on nineteen different factors. The following conclusions can be drawn from the hypothetical figures:

1 Two or three of the markets are clearly more suitable for the company than the others. Even if it would be ridiculous to take small differences in total score too seriously, markets A, E and H are far ahead of the others, while markets D and G are extremely poor.

2 It is rewarding to analyse how the various markets differ. Market A, for example, scores because of rising sales in the past, favourable competitive conditions and suitable sales and distribution facilities. It is notable, however, in its lack of long-term growth prospects unlike Markèt E. The latter clearly is a fine long-term prospect, but suf-

fers from being different from the company's current production and distribution facilities. Market H, on the other hand, shows no growth prospects and has also had no past growth unlike A. It scores highly by being very suitable for the company's current resources and would benefit from the company's name and brand images.

If the above conclusions are accepted, it follows that it is possible on the basis of the screen to eliminate the completely unsuitable markets and to divide the possibly suitable ones by time, and thus begin to formulate a short- and long-term programme. Thus Market H could present very quick low investment opportunities, Market A would similarly be short-term, while Market E could only be included in a long-term programme.

Once the above conclusions are made, the markets which have been singled out can be analysed in depth in a way which is not possible on a crude screen and doubtless a larger proportion will still be eliminated at a later stage.

I hope, however, that the examples have demonstrated the value of the quick sieve at an early stage, however crude. Not only does it ensure that the broadest possible spectrum of opportunities is taken into consideration. It also enables the company to concentrate its attention at a very early stage on a relatively small number of opportunities.

The ability to differentiate between markets and projects at a very early stage is extremely important for the company and it is not easy to achieve this discipline. In practice most companies have a large number of development projects at various stages which they hesitate to kill or postpone, as there is usually some reason why each one has potential promise. Yet because the company hesitates to eliminate the majority of such projects, it is likely to find it difficult to progress any satisfactorily. For example, if the R and D department have, say, forty projects going through the works and if another twenty or thirty are being studied from the market and research angles, the company must suffer from development indigestion. Few if any projects come out at the end of the line and progress is extremely slow because of the diffusion of attention and resources on so many projects.

A quick screen enables the company to abandon or at any rate postpone most of the projects. It may then go on by concentrating on, say, only about a dozen of the most promising ones and the speed with which these can be tackled would be a revelation to most companies. The early isolation of marketing opportunities, even subject to later validation, is a crucial ingredient in a successful development programme.

eight progress up to national launch

step-by-step approach

Once the suitable market has been identified and the opportunities have been defined, the development process has, of course, only just begun. One now embarks on the tortuous road leading eventually up to national launch if the project survives all the obstacles in its path.

There are varying attitudes towards the development process starting at this stage. At one end of the scale is the painstaking approach. So many new products fail, so it is vital to measure all the important factors, even if this takes a long time. By the end the product will be so acceptable both to the trade and to the consumer that the painstaking process will be found worthwhile.

At the other end of the scale is the opposite approach. Development can be compared with the sex life of an elephant —at first there is much noise normally in high quarters and then nothing happens for a terribly long time. Because it is so easy to find reasons for more research all the time and because the research normally gives only imperfect answers, this school of thought firmly believes that one must move very fast to produce a product and with the minimum of research launch it in a small test area, say in a town. At this stage the company learns about the attitudes towards the product in the market, and changes in the product and in its marketing can be made and tested in realistic conditions.

As usual the right answer lies somewhere in between the two extremes. A research programme is certainly worthwhile if the risk and the opportunity justify it, but it is impossible to take the risk element out of a development project. In the end, judgment will still be needed on whether to go ahead or not and there will still be important assumptions to make which research has not covered.

It may seem possible to research every important point in a large project, but in practice this is not realistic. In a recent project a great deal of time and money had been spent on formulation of assumptions and on research to validate them. When it was realized, however, that the majority of assumptions had still not been validated, the possibility of doing so was considered and it was found that the research would take another three years, while the cost of it would be astronomical!

At the same time, to move very fast to a town test often means taking important and expensive decisions to reach that stage. A pilot plant may be necessary, the sales force effort, though limited, must affect the sales of the company's other products and a number of town tests at the same time would take up much of the sales force's resources. Similarly there would be expensive use of R and D because very fast progress means that there would be little possibility of cutting the number of projects once they had been selected for development, so they would all go through R and D. Moreover, the marketing budgets even in a town can run to many thousands of pounds if one considers the advertising, trade and consumer promotions, point of sale material and the research necessary to measure the test. Finally, much management time would need to be spent on each project of this nature which could otherwise be allocated to items of more immediate profit to the company.

I believe, therefore, that the best approach is to prepare a programme of progress up to the launch based on a number of steps or hurdles that the project needs to overcome one by one. It is agreed that the path up to the launch is a hazardous one, so the hurdles need to be overcome in turn if the project is to progress. They will vary according to the project. For example, a major and complicated market entry would clearly merit a much more comprehensive programme than a relatively safe range extension which could well justify quick progress to a national launch without preliminary test marketing.

In principle, the initial steps should be inexpensive. They should largely cover areas where assumptions can be made. Then as the project surmounts more and more hurdles and so becomes increasingly viable, there is growing justification in spending money to validate the assumptions through market research and in development of the product through R and D.

Such a step by step approach provides management with a pre-designed number of cut-off points, so that a project needs to progress strictly on its merits if it is to reach the final stages. Yet it need not be slow where speed is important. In practice it has proved itself time and time again as an important discipline in new product development.

the steps

There is no magic list which will apply in every case. Nevertheless a typical list is given below and it should be useful for adaptation to a company's particular needs.

It is assumed that the company has carried out a screening operation, as described in the previous chapter, and that as a result it has narrowed down the list of suitable opportunities to be examined further and to be progressed up to national launch if they continue to look promising. In the circumstances the steps which would follow are:

1. PRELIMINARY FINANCIAL EVALUATION

The screening process is unlikely to include detailed financial evaluations for every possible opportunity screened. It is important, therefore, to test the financial implications of the short list of selected opportunities in relation to the financial criteria laid down by the company.

At this stage, it is unlikely that much factual information is available, so there is need for the usual assumptions, particularly on such points as cost of goods and cost of plant. Other costs such as distribution, sales force, general overheads, etc. can often be estimated reasonably accurately on the basis of comparisons with the company's other products.

The market trends and shares which the company is likely to obtain can also be extremely difficult to forecast and a careful look at the particular market is necessary, to see what has happened on such occasions in the past. The company's performance in past development products should also be a useful pointer.

At times, the market does not exist at all or is completely undeveloped. In such cases it is necessary to consider the markets which will be affected by the new one. For example, if one were to assess the market for the first hovercraft, there would be, of course, no competition, but one would have to consider instead the market for all other types of transport which would be relevant and forecast the share of this wide market which the hovercraft could achieve at each point in time.

Once the best possible assumptions have been made and the ensuing sales and profits have been calculated, the estimated rate of profit, the investment time and the return on capital employed can be compared with the company criteria.

It may be thought that all this is not worth the paper it is written on at this stage, as so few of the figures are likely to be more than informed guesses. Such criticism is reasonable, but wrong.

In practice it has been found that, however rough, the financial calculations have been invaluable from the earliest stage, so long as the assumptions are clearly recognized and validated as the project progresses. In many cases the early forecasts done by experienced executives can be surprisingly accurate and, in any case, by including them at several stages of a project, the company stresses the importance of the financial aspect— after all nothing else matters. This attitude is all too rare among the majority of marketing executives, certainly in the U.K.

Many of the opportunities will founder at the first financial hurdle, if the figures built into the forecasts are realistic and not over-enthusiastic in a misguided attempt to make the project succeed.

If the project looks financially unsound, it must not go on in the hope that 'something might turn up'. The earlier it is killed the better, in order to save time and money and to channel the company's resources to better projects.

If, however, a project has passed the screen and is financially attractive in terms of the company's criteria, it needs to go on to the next stage. In most cases the opportunity till now has only been defined very broadly, e.g. the refrigerator market or paperback books. The company now needs to establish how it can take advantage of the opportunity which has been uncovered—how it should tackle the refrigerator or paperback market, what reasons will the trade and the consumer have for buying its refrigerators or paperbacks rather than the ones already on the market. There is need for a product concept.

2. PRODUCT CONCEPT

The broad policy for presenting the new product to the public and to the trade will depend, of course, very much on the type of product and on the market. For example, General Foods were able to obtain a large share of the U.K. instant coffee market simply because they were the second major manufacturer after Nestlé. Their product was very similar and there was nothing in their marketing policy to establish a clear distinction except possibly the slogan 'America's favourite coffee'. Yet when such companies as Lyons and Brooke Bond tried to enter the market later, they failed to secure an important share. The market had no room for more major brands unless possibly they could establish a very distinctive appeal—a most difficult task. Thus General Foods did not need a distinctive product concept at the time of their entry, whereas Lyons and Brooke Bond certainly did later on.

It is becoming, however, more and more vital for new products to have distinctive concepts. Those who do not have such a concept either fail or are particularly vulnerable to competition.

Yet it is not always possible to find a concept which is important enough for the consumer. For example, in the later 1950's a glucose drink was launched in the U.K. which had some technical advantages over Lucozade. There were found, however, not to be important for the consumer and the product failed in test market.

Similarly, the great effort by Campbell Soups in the U.K. has proved extremely expensive not because the condensed idea was not acceptable, but because it was not important enough. The consumer was happy with Heinz and had no reason to eat another similar soup even if it might have some advantages. Paper tissues, on the other hand, had very great advantages in convenience; the public accepted them readily and paid relatively high prices for them.

It is important, therefore, to assess at this stage not only the brand loyalty in the market being examined, but also the level of satisfaction with the current product types and the possibility of product differentiation. Moreover, in a large market, the concept may arise out of market segmentation. For example baby toiletries have achieved some success in the large toiletry market through such a segmentation process.

The product concept can arise from real innovation or from lessons learnt from competitors' innovation. Thus Batchelors' Vesta range has been a successful concept for a product first in the field. McVities, on the other hand, were late in the prepackaged cake field but could learn from Lyons and Cadbury's experience to improve their own products. This approach is particularly common with consumer durables which so often have initial teething troubles and so give the opportunity to the second company in the market to produce a superior product.

Whether there is much consumer research on the market being studied or not, again assumptions need normally to be made at this stage on current attitudes towards existing products and the direction towards which a new concept should turn. It is normally worth validating, however, the concepts found, even by means of a few group discussions, which are cheap and often very rewarding.

It should then be possible to see whether a method has been found of exploiting the selected opportunity which gives the consumer and the trade an important reason for buying the product. If there is no such concept, the product should be dropped until such a concept can be found. If there is one, we can go on to the next stage.

3. OUTLINE MARKETING PLAN

The opportunity has been isolated. It seems financially sound. A strong concept has been found. Now is the time to make the preliminary marketing plan. This should concentrate particularly on the product—its physical attributes, sizes, prices, etc. and on the product concept translated into a marketing and an advertising strategy.

Such a preliminary plan will serve as background to the brief to R and D. It should be reasonably straightforward at this stage to tell R and D that they should aim to develop a product with certain well defined attributes and with detailed costings to achieve. Even if in practice the costings are found to be impossible to achieve, as obviously can happen, a definite costing brief in line with the marketing plan ensures that the final outcome of R and D activity is as close to the needs of the market as possible.

At times it has been found useful to produce advertising material even at this early stage both to test the concept and to serve as a brief to the laboratory. For example, in a market where advertising was a dominant factor, it was decided that it would be impossible to establish the concept and the resulting advertising policy without actually producing the advertisement. This was done in the form of a Press layout and formed an integral part of the outline marketing plan which was passed over to R and D. In another case three different advertising campaigns were prepared illustrating different concepts and product characteristics. In this way the most suitable concept was found and the relevant campaign was part of the brief to R and D.

4. LABORATORY WORK

The stages so far have necessarily been a little theoretical and 'airy fairy'. Now comes the acid test consisting of the translation of all paper work into physical development work.

Companies vary in their attitude towards the relationship between marketing, planning and technical development. Despite the general trend towards marketing orientation, many companies, probably the majority, find it difficult to develop new concepts, particularly in markets new to the company. This means that this factor needs to be taken into account and development outside the experience of the R and D department must be kept to a minimum.

On the other hand, there are marketing companies which believe that in this day and age there should be no important technical problems in developing marketing concepts. If R and D do not have the necessary experience, there must be others with suitable experience whose services can be bought.

Some concepts can in fact present R and D with very difficult technical problems which are found to be either insoluble or need very long development time. The price/performance relationship is of course crucial, because it is no use producing, say, the most perfect dishwasher possible for £400 if one wants a fairly high turnover. R and D is and must be a series of compromises between price and performance and it is vital that the technicians should have a detailed understanding of the relative importance of price and performance in each case. Too often unnecessary qualities are built into the product and so make the costings impossible. Perhaps an integral part of the training programme for a R and D technician should be a few weeks on the road, preferably selling new products!

It is also possible that the concept required in the marketing plan is unrealistic but there are others which can be translated into physical products and which seem interesting. Close liaison between R and D and the marketing executives is clearly essential and much flexibility may be necessary.

If R and D cannot progress the project satisfactorily, then clearly it dies at this stage. If, however, they develop new product formulations or prototypes, it is important for the relevant product development or marketing executives to check that the R and D work in fact conforms with the original or with the altered brief. If it is found that this is so, it is now possible to proceed to the next stage, i.e. to tests with consumers so that the latter are given the chance to show whether the company has been right in assessing their requirements. Product testing follows with all its ramifications.

5. CONSUMER TESTING CLEARANCE

However good the preliminary planning, however good the translation of the planning into a physical product, there must be very good reasons for not finding out the consumer's reaction towards the product. None of us can represent the consumer adequately enough to avoid consumer research at some stage of the development process.

It is easy to say that there is no point if the product is well proven. For example, some years ago a large international company refused to spend a small sum of money to test a new product among the public because, as they said, 'the ingredients and the formulation are identical to everyone else's'. They did not deserve to succeed and they did not. The product was a dismal failure.

Very recently another company had developed a food product over many years which everyone was convinced was much superior to the brand leader. There was much urgency to launch and it really did not seem worthwhile to test the new product. The test did finally take place as a form of insurance and the result was an eye-opener. The consumers declared against the new product almost unanimously on every factor measured. The project was killed and a calamity averted.

The consumer testing is required for two main reasons:

1 To check that the concept, as represented by the product, is acceptable.
2 To check that the product performance meets the required objectives and that there are no important negative answers.

At times the concept will have already been validated before the technical development stage, but the consumer finds it difficult to grasp a concept if the actual product is not available, particularly if the concept is new or unfamiliar. Moreover the actual product as developed may cause different reactions from those aroused by the concept on its own. I recommend therefore that while the product is tested the concept should be validated at the same time. The extra cost tends to be relatively low.

As far as the actual product testing is concerned, this is particularly useful in a negative form. According to current practice the consumer is normally asked for his reaction to the new product in comparison with at least one other already on the market and the products are not labelled in any way. Such comparisons can lead to misleading results if interpreted too literally because in real life the label and everything associated with it can have a great impact on the consumer.

For example, in the case of two food products, 'blind' consumer testing always shows no statistically significant difference between them. In actual sales, however, one of them outsells the other by about 9:1 simply because of its much better known name. In another example product A always beats product B about 60:40 only to be outsold by about 7:1. Again a strong name and 'brand image' cause the difference.

It follows, therefore, that a score in relation to the brand leader of say 45:55 cannot be used at all for forecasting the respective market shares if the consumer is not aware of the two products' identity. One can only conclude that the new product is very little, if at all, inferior as a product, though its consumer acceptance in the market place could be very much lower than the well established brand leader. The results can only be used very broadly to answer the questions which only the consumer can answer regarding the new product, however hard the company tries to answer the questions on his or her behalf.

Very often the consumer testing shows criticisms of points which the company has either overlooked or has not considered important. For example, confusing instructions for use can destroy the new product and are nearly always improved following consumer testing. A small blemish in the finish could be the one point which consumers notice when testing furniture. Lack of a parcel rack may bias them against a new car. The first appearance of the product could prejudice them against it even though it provides important consumer benefits.

Certainly the consumer cannot be underestimated. It has been shown time and time again that by their actions consumers notice slight changes in products which even technical experts do not notice. And the consumer may not agree with the expert. I well remember the case of a product which was technically considered superior to all those on the market at the time, yet the consumers voted strongly against the theoretical improvement. The technical director could rant as much as he liked that the public were wrong. It was far easier to change the product than the strongly held views of many millions of people!

If the consumer verdict is unfavourable and it is not practicable to change the product accordingly to maintain a distinctive advantage over the competition, then again the natural decision is to suspend the project. If the changes are important and can be made, it is usually useful to retest the revised product to ensure that the revisions satisfy the consumer. Eventually the situation is reached when the consumer is satisfied—and this can happen, of course, following the first testing. Once the consumer testing clearance is obtained, the project appears promising indeed and is a crucial step nearer the launch.

6. SALES FORCE CLEARANCE

Broad plans would already have been made regarding the sales operation for the new product. It is necessary, however, to examine the matter closely at this stage.

Either a new sales operation is needed, which takes considerable time to put in motion, so planning must begin now, or the new product is going to be handled by the existing sales force. If so, the needs of the new product have to be examined with regard both to its own sales and to those of the other lines.

For example, a product can be developed which in theory can easily be handled by the company's current sales force, but in practice the latter cannot give it adequate time, either because they have no capacity for new products or because the new product seems very unimportant in comparison with the current ones.

The questions of sales force capacity and attitude need therefore to be carefully studied, particularly as in this area there is great scope for efficiency. In many product fields, for example, one company uses a sales force of only, say sixty men, whereas its nearest competitor may have 300. In some markets it may be possible to have a very small sales force, e.g. in chemist goods because of the importance of two or three organizations and of wholesalers all of whom can be contacted even by one man. On the other hand there is also much scope for miscalculation as sales force costs can represent an important proportion of the new product's costings. In one recent U.K. launch the merchandising requirements of the new product were badly underestimated and this was the main factor in turning a promising launch into a loss situation. It does not follow, of course, that the smallest possible sales force is necessarily the best for the new product. It may be decided that emphasis will be put on the selling and merchandising operation as an important competitive factor in the launch of the new product as McVitie did in the launch of their cakes. This needs, however, to be very much a conscious operation and must be costed into the product.

Let us assume that the broad plans for selling the new product are confirmed at this stage after detailed study. Sales force clearance is obtained.

7. LEGAL CLEARANCE

Now that the project has reached an advanced stage, it is necessary to check on the various legal implications. The product name or names would probably have been provisionally agreed in the preliminary marketing plan, but the time has come to ensure their registration, if this has not already been done.

In addition, final legal clearance is needed regarding the product formulation, the concept and the packaging and labelling requirements. In many product fields the legal question is crucial, e.g. in the development of medical proprietary products, and a detailed assessment of the relevant legal position may at times be needed much earlier, before the product has been developed.

8. PRODUCT CLEARANCE

The product for the consumer tests may have been produced on a pilot plant or it may have been no more than a prototype, e.g. in the case of a consumer durable. In either case full scale production on a normal plant needs to be carefully considered at this stage. This affects not only costings but also such factors as the product's physical properties and the quality control needed to achieve a consistent standard.

For example, a large U.K. company recently launched a new consumer durable which found a very high level of consumer acceptance both for the concept and for the product when it was produced in very small batches. Once the product was launched, however, it was proved impossible to maintain adequate quality control within the costings and so the product had to be withdrawn.

It is necessary, therefore, to make a very detailed study of the likely conditions in a full production run including plant costs, capacity, quality control and the costings at different levels of output with a breakdown of fixed and of variable costs.

Experience in this crucial area affects the accuracy of the study. Some companies, even large ones, find it very difficult to estimate the likely cost of goods of a new product and so either the costs of production are in practice far above forecast, leading to disaster, or the estimates are so pessimistic that every project is turned down because of its insufficient profit margins. Other companies, however, have learnt from the launch of numerous new products and from study of past forecasts in relation to the actual figures and are able to produce reasonably accurate estimates. This is obviously an important advantage and possibly many companies could improve by acquiring greater experience in this field. For example, a company would learn a good deal by carrying out an exercise assuming that it had to launch the products which it in fact has been marketing for some time and so could compare its forecasts with the actual figures.

If the product study confirms the broad estimates made previously so that the project still looks promising, one can now move to the last development stages.

9. FINAL MARKETING CLEARANCE

By now it should be possible to take a detailed look at the whole operation. Market research may be necessary to answer a few crucial questions, but otherwise the links in the chain should be coming together.

The financial side can be treated more accurately than before and so the project needs to be re-appraised to see whether it is viable. If it is, final decisions should be taken on the product itself, on its pricing, its packaging, its distribution, its selling and, in general, on its complete marketing plans.

At this point the company needs to decide finally whether to go ahead or not, unless new developments take place later which would affect the decision.

10. TEST MARKETING CLEARANCE

It is recognized that all the planning in the world cannot re-place actual experience in the market place, so it is not sur-prising that many companies automatically test market new products in an area, to limit their risk.

This is reasonable, so long as it is not automatic. There are occasions when the advantages of quick action and of resulting surprise must outweigh the reasons for test marketing. More-over, if the plant for national distribution is the same as for a test area, as is generally the case with consumer durables, there may be little financial reason for test marketing, unless the marketing expenditure is particularly important.

Timing can be crucial in certain product fields, and so an immediate national launch can at times be advisable, so long as the risks are examined closely. For example, Mars who had developed the U.K. instant potato market with their brand Yeoman found themselves suddenly being challenged in various areas by Cadbury's with Smash. It was probably right for Mars to retaliate by launching nationally a new brand, Dine, before Cadbury's could expand nationally. Similarly, Gibbs launched nationally their fluoride toothpaste to fore-stall Procter and Gamble who had been test marketing their brand, Crest, for many months.

In general, however, an area test market is an extremely useful last step before national launch because it enables the company to acquire experience of the new product in the mar-ket and to have its national plans validated in practice.

Many new products fail in test market. Those which suc-ceed in meeting the objectives laid down are now ready for the last hurdle—national marketing.

11. NATIONAL MARKETING

By now, the company should know a great deal about the mar-ket in most cases, and the risks of national marketing, though not eliminated, must be very much diminished.

Nevertheless, it is important that the national launch and the plans for future national marketing should be regarded as the last part of the development process. Otherwise it is too easy to make decisions altering the total project and possibly making it unviable.

For example, Company D developed carefully a product up to national launch. At this stage during and after the launch the company increased their marketing expenditure considerably, because of short term pressures, and the project became financially unsound. Under the pressure of events, the company did not take into account the financial plan prepared and agreed during the development programme.

Company E launched a number of products in one market, covering several market sectors, following much preparatory development, including test market. Yet while it was decided to launch the total range nationally on consideration of the total test results, not enough attention was paid to the individual market sectors. Otherwise some of the products would not have been launched, which later proved a severe burden to the company.

Company F also carried out a serious development programme which justified national launch. After the launch, however, it was found that the existing sales force was not adequate to handle the new products, so considerable sales force expansion took place. This led to serious financial problems as the costings did not allow for additional salesmen and the new products had to be withdrawn eventually.

The above examples illustrate the need to consider the national launch and subsequent marketing in the light of the development plans. These often need to be amended, but any changes must be made consciously and their effect on the costings must be calculated carefully. This sounds obvious, but too many companies in the heat of battle take quick decisions without making such considerations and often regret their decisions later.

nine the creative element

importance of the creative spark

The development process as described in the previous chapter may give the impression of a complicated set of procedures at the end of which the new product emerges and is bound to make millions for the company.

Unfortunately, or perhaps fortunately, life is not like this, otherwise it would be very dull if a reasonable set of procedures could ensure a success. In fact they can only help. There is no substitute, however, even in the age of marketing 'science' and of computers, for the old-fashioned creative spark.

An interesting argument took place in the columns of the *Financial Times* [1] between Anthony Harris and me. He argued that the idea was everything and the only successful innovations were those based on a striking new idea. My argument, on the other hand, was that there is no such thing as a good idea in a vacuum. It is only good for a particular company, so it needs to be evolved as part of the planning process.

It is probable in fact that both arguments are right. There is vital need for the creative spark in the new product or service, but I am still convinced that it is useless and even dangerous in isolation. It needs to be related to the company's resources and plans.

the idea in the development process

The place of the concept in the total development process has already been outlined in the previous chapter. Ideally, the creative idea should fit in as follows:

1. *Financial Times*, July 25 and August 1, 1967.

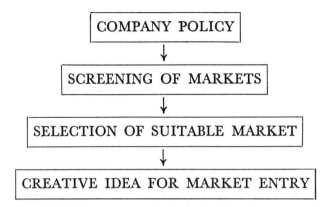

Yet too often creative ideas do not wait until the correct stage in the development has been reached. Either the mind is completely barren then or ideas suddenly erupt at any time.

It would be easy to eliminate all ideas which do not fit in exactly with the correct sequence. This would be stupid, however, as important opportunities would be missed just for the sake of a set of procedures. It is important, therefore, that the company should allow for and encourage ideas at any time.

An alternative evaluation process would then be necessary, starting with the idea. In fact the process would be a reversal of the normal one, as follows:

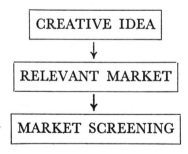

If the idea seems interesting, it should be related to a particular market, data on which would be collected. The market would then be screened in comparison with other markets which the company has examined, so that it can be decided whether it is or is not of interest in relation to the others. If it is, one would then proceed to financial evaluation, laboratory work, product testing, etc.

search for ideas

In practice, there is often a dearth of good ideas and various methods are used to find them. The main ones are the following:

1. STUDY OF COMPANY'S PRODUCTS ABROAD

International companies often have a large number of products which they only market in one or two countries. It is not unusual for such a company to have up to, say, 200 products of which not more than 20–30 appear in any one country. What is surprising is that in many cases little or no effort is made to co-ordinate all these products and examine any ideas which could be applied to other countries, although the situation is changing, following the recent growth of international marketing structures.

Examination of all the company's products can often lead to exciting product concepts, particularly if successes in more advanced economies such as the United States or Sweden can be applied to the U.K. Normally there is a great advantage if the product already exists and is marketed by the company as there will be expertise available, so long as the differences between countries are realized.

2. STUDY OF OTHER PRODUCTS

Unashamed plagiarism of products marketed abroad by other companies can also pay off. The Japanese boom is evidence of this in many markets, though more recently they have also led in many technological innovations.

Travel abroad to study latest consumer and trade trends, attendance at international fairs and exhibitions and finally study of foreign literature will serve to provide the necessary information and source of ideas.

3. CONSUMER GROUP DISCUSSIONS

Once the market has been defined, it is possible to hold group discussions among the selected market target to find ideas and discuss them. In practice such discussions are often not particularly fruitful, because the consumer finds it difficult to visualize what does not exist and is too much influenced by the current products in the market.

4. BRAINSTORMING SESSIONS

Brainstorming sessions, if well planned, can be extremely rewarding. They should consist not only of executives concerned with the project but also of some who know nothing about it and so can tackle it with a fresh outlook uninhibited by knowledge.

In practice the session leader should outline the background briefly and possibly stimulate the group with a few initial ideas—even fanciful ones. It is important to let the participants give vent to their imagination and to allow them to put up suggestions, however wild they may be. If every suggestion is met by the reaction: 'it cannot be done', the session soon ends without useful results.

If, however, the right atmosphere and approach are encouraged, such sessions have been found to be absolutely invaluable in practice and to produce a wealth of ideas, which, after careful selection subsequently, can often form the basis for product concepts. If there is a problem in such sessions, it is that they produce too many ideas rather than too few; there is certainly no lack of ideas.

For example, Company G was seeking to take advantage of its very considerable facilities for technological innovation by developing a number of new products representing concepts not existing anywhere in the world. After a market study and screening which isolated the most suitable markets for the company, a series of brainstorming sessions proved to be the most useful method of finding the large number of completely new concepts which was required.

5. SPECTRUM ANALYSIS

Formal procedures can be used for finding market gaps. A useful one is to examine all the important factors in the market and range the existing products according to these factors. For example, if one were to examine the low calory foods market one factor would be their appearance.

Existing products could well be ranged as follows:

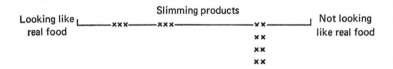

Thus most slimming products do not look like real food. Other scales could be fattening/non-fattening, eaten by men/women, masochistic/not masochistic, etc.

When all the relevant factors are examined the gaps can be put together almost as if on an overlay and gap combinations can lead to interesting concepts.

There are computer programmes catering for this technique, owing to the number of variables which can be used.

6. GRID ANALYSIS

Another method of finding product concepts is by segmenting market groups and activities. For examples, if one wants to find a concept for bread, a simple grid could be built as follows:

BREAD

	men	women	children	young	old	middle class	lower class	bachelors	families	weight watchers	non-weight watchers
For sand-wiches											
For toast											
For break-fast											
Flavo-ured											
Raft for spreads											
Cheap											
Expen-sive											
Filling											
Not filling											

Clearly one can add as many characteristics as one wants to on such a grid. What it does provide is a disciplined method for putting down on paper various combinations and again computers can be used to good effect if there is a large number of combinations.

the problem of keeping creative lead
Whether the company is an innovator or an imitator, it faces the serious problem that these days it is relatively simple for competitors to copy its products in a short time.

This is naturally an important factor in development, because if a company spends much time and money in improving on existing products only to be copied by the competition within months, then there is a danger that competitive activity simply cancels out the development effort of every company.

It follows, therefore, that the creative idea should not only incorporate an important product advantage but should also be either exclusive to the company or impossible to copy quickly for various reasons. The problem is particularly acute in fast-moving packaged goods where a company, if it really wants to move, can often introduce a new product in a matter of weeks.

Patents naturally protect the innovator, but in many cases there is nothing patentable in the new product or if there is a patent an alternative solution can be quickly found.

It follows, therefore, that one approach in the search for creative ideas is to start by listing all the possible attributes which are exclusive to the company, to see whether they can be applied to the new product. This may seem a reversion to the old fashioned production-orientation, but in fact it is simply use of the company's resources for sound marketing reasons.

If exclusive concepts cannot be found, one may be successful in establishing enough lead time before the competition can copy. There are still technological processes which cannot be copied overnight. The source of raw materials for the products can be contracted for in its entirety, so that the competition would need to create new supply sources. One may still be able to count on specialist plant which may need 2–3 years to be obtained. Study of the competition's management could suggest that they would not move for years. Points such as these play an important role in the selection of the creative idea.

the artificial concept

At times it is possible to build into a product a concept which can be made exclusive to it through advertising even though it is not exclusive as far as physical characteristics are concerned. For example, the words 'good for you' could be applied to almost any product, but having been used for Guinness over many years they have been really appropriated by the product. Thus the goodness concept has been the main reason for the product's success over the years.

Similarly in product fields such as cigarettes or cosmetics, where it is so difficult to find a physical product difference, the personality imparted to the product can in fact become an important product advantage. Thus the approach chosen for Strand, as the cigarette which one can enjoy even when alone, could have been used for almost any cigarette brand, but once it was applied to Strand, it was very difficult to copy.

As it happened, the concept misfired but there was no denying its strength even though it was completely artificial.

Naturally it is preferable to market the product on the basis of an actual product difference, but if this is impractical the possibility of an artificial concept should not be disregarded from the earliest stages. Even if it can be copied, the first product to use it must have an advantage and what evidence there is suggests that in most consumer goods fields the followers find it hard and relatively expensive to imitate the concept subsequently.

ten financial evaluation

financial appraisal in the development process

The importance of financial evaluation has already been mentioned and is self-evident. A development project either will or will not be financially beneficial to the company and this one factor will determine whether it is worthwhile proceeding at each stage of the operation.

This means not only that the company should have standard financial criteria laid down, so that each project can be related to them as well as to other opportunities which may be open to the company at that particular time. It is also vital that systems should be built into the development process enabling the company to assess the financial viability of a project at each stage.

Too often companies make such an evaluation, even very thoroughly, usually taking up much of the accountants' time, but do it once only as it is such a major operation. It is not sufficiently recognized that the figures at the end of twenty or thirty pages of calculations, even if blessed with such impressive names as discounted cash flow, net present value, equivalent mean investment period, etc. are only as good or as bad as the original assumptions on which the figures are based. And these assumptions can change very frequently, sometimes every few days, as the project develops and more is discovered about the market, the production process and the selling operation.

The U.S. study of new products conducted by the New Products Institute Inc. has already been mentioned. When the 200 large U.S. manufacturers of packaged consumer products were asked how the costs which they actually incurred in introducing their new products compared with their estimates, as many as 70 per cent answered that they were higher, 6 per cent said they were lower and 24 per cent that they were on target.

Similarly in the U.K. I am convinced that costs generally rise as the project develops. New plant is not utilized in practice as efficiently as preliminary estimates would indicate, raw material prices may fluctuate and, if the company is in a new market, there is not enough experience in the first few years of how to buy most profitably; the packaging could be changed at the last minute requiring a more expensive material; the planned marketing expenditure levels are found not to be sufficient; more salesmen and greater trade incentives are needed than was forecast in order to reach adequate distribution levels. All these and many other such events are only too common and some provision must be made for their occurrence. Otherwise even a most promising project can easily become a horrible failure if constant track is not kept of the financial changes in the project and of their implications with regard to its viability.

For example, one company recently launched a new product without foreseeing that the sales force needed to devote a considerable amount of time to it if it were to be successful. This was realized in the test market, but the company still went ahead without revising its costings and in the event the product was most disappointing because the company could not afford to give it the necessary attention at the point of sale.

Another company made no attempt to forecast competitors' reaction to its new product and so did not cater for this in the planned marketing expenditure. So when the product was launched and the competition took retaliatory action, the company was forced to support its new product at a rate which made it completely uneconomic and soon led to its withdrawal.

In another case, a company made a very detailed evaluation

which showed that a new product was extremely promising and, having decided to go ahead, changed the journey cycle without examining the effect of this on the total project. Already in the test market evidence could be found that the project was unprofitable as it required a far larger sales force than anticipated, but the company only saw that the targeted market share was reached and so launched nationally with very unfortunate results.

Moreover it is possible that genuine mistakes can be made in financial calculations, if the company relies on one evaluation only. It may be thought that this point cannot be important if a reasonably efficient and sophisticated company is involved in a new product launch, but in fact large international corporations have suffered disasters simply because someone put in the decimal point in the wrong place or through another such error.

I hope, therefore, that the case is made for very frequent financial appraisals and re-appraisals and for ones readily understood within the company. If a procedure is even 20 per cent less efficient in evaluating a project, it is preferable if it is also simpler, so that:

1 Everyone can understand it.
2 There is less scope for errors.
3 It is quick to use and so can be done frequently.

There are signs that companies have improved their methods of financial evaluation in recent years. Certainly the investment incentives survey conducted in 1965 by the C.B.I. showed that the large companies were more aware than before of accurate techniques and took taxation and investment allowances into consideration to a greater extent than before.

In a company with a number of development projects being progressed at the same time it may be advisable to have an accountant as a member of the development team, to ensure that this aspect of the development process is given its due importance. This would ensure that the accountant is not just the man in the accounts department whose help is suddenly invoked when intricate financial problems arise. He should instead be in continuous touch with the project and have a complete understanding of marketing, the risks and opportunities involved and of the company's resources and needs for the future. He needs in fact to be a well-rounded commercial executive with specialist financial experience. Without this broad experience and constant exposure to the company's general position how can he appreciate the implications of the figures he is asked to calculate?

Many companies will testify to the number of projects which have been wrongly evaluated because the Board accepted the judgment of an accountant who did not really understand the figures on which he had to pronounce. Too often promising projects have been abandoned because long-term trends were not examined and the accountant insisted on an immediate pay-out. Alternatively, some projects have gone ahead to disastrous conclusions because the accountant did not realize the importance of such elements as the competition or trade reaction or consumer preferences.

In this aspect, as in so many others, the attitude of the company management is crucial. It is pointless to have efficient systems and people in order to evaluate a project if the Board, or whoever makes the final decision, cannot use the evaluation. This sounds obvious, but needs saying, because in practice many of the senior executives in the U.K. are still afraid of figures. How many use and understand even the simpler forms of discounted cash flow in order to decide on important investment decisions? As A. P. Hichens[1] says, discounted cash flow was described in detail in 1951, seventeen years ago, yet many companies still treat it very gingerly as a newfangled gadget.

Yet surely a company's management has few more important functions than to decide on the most profitable methods of investing the company's resources. In this connection, I suggest that a Board of Management should investigate its procedure and organization for evaluating new products and

1. 'Risks and Discounts', A. P. Hichens, *Financial Times*, July 9, 1968.

acquisitions and should ensure that both procedure and organization are the most efficient and the most suitable in relation to the company's needs. If some self-education is necessary in the process to make full use of these procedures, the company can only benefit.

evaluation procedures

Companies use a number of different procedures. The main ones can be listed as follows: [1]

1 Payback period.
2 Return on capital.
3 Discounted cash flow.

1. PAYBACK PERIOD

The company simply calculates the number of years necessary to recover the cost of the project. Usually depreciation is ignored and it can be calculated both before and after tax.

The system has the virtue of great simplicity and is completely intelligible to everyone in the company. It has some serious drawbacks, however. Even if the implication of investment incentives and of taxation is considered, the method does not take into account the earning life of the project. Thus a project on which the company recovers its investment after five years, which has an expectation of subsequent profits for another ten years, ranks equal to another project which also leads to investment recovery after five years, but which is likely to die shortly afterwards.

Moreover, no allowance is made for the timing of expenditure and income. Clearly the company benefits if expenditure is delayed as long as possible while income comes in as soon as possible, but the payback system does not recognize this factor. If two projects to be assessed had the estimates shown below, they would be ranked equal.

1. *Discounted Cash Flow and Corporate Planning*, A. M. Alfred, published by Woolwich Polytechnic, July 1964.
Investment Appraisal, H.M.S.O., 1967.

| | PROJECT A | | PROJECT B | |
| | £'000 | | £'000 | |
	Outflow	Inflow	Outflow	Inflow
Year 1	50	5	20	10
Year 2	10	10	20	20
Year 3	10	55	10	20
Total	70	70	50	50

In both cases it takes three years for cumulative break even to be achieved, but no financial genius is needed to see that Project B seems better than Project A where the company does not recover much of the investment until the third year.

Thus the payback period method can be positively misleading and should not be used on its own although it may have a role to play in conjunction with other methods which compensate for its disadvantages.

2. RETURN ON CAPITAL

Return on capital criteria and methods are probably the most frequently used, but again they present a number of very important disadvantages. There are problems of definition. The profit return normally varies over the years, so should the figures used be an average or the one achieved in the final year? If depreciation is allowed for, it is usually at an artificial rate which is different from the company's investment incentives, while the impact of taxation again is normally not included. Even if the procedure involves accurate estimates of taxation and investment incentives, the two major snags of the payback period method are repeated:

1 The profitable life of the project is not taken into consideration.
2 The evaluation rates £1 in the first year as having the same value as £1 five or more years later.

It must be concluded, therefore, that the return on capital method can again be misleading and would be dangerous to use in isolation.

3. DISCOUNTED CASH FLOW

Discounted Cash Flow, or D.C.F. as it is commonly called, has already been mentioned as a modern method from which many companies shy away. It certainly has the disadvantage that it does not represent a familiar process and a considerable amount of calculation is involved.

In practice, however, there are standard computer programmes which can be used to take the drudgery out of the calculations and the system has the great advantage, as the name implies, that allowance is made for the time when the cash inflows and outflows occur by discounting the value of cash the further away it is removed from the present.

There have been a number of books on the subject describing both U.K.[1] and U.S.[2] practice. Basically, however, the system combines and treats in the same way both capital expenditure on plant and equipment and operational costs whereas companies usually distinguish between the two and often achieve misleading results. For example, Bodroghy[3] quotes in this connection the interesting example of coalmining where it is usual to regard the cost of sinking a mine shaft as capital while the cost of tunnels is considered an operational cost. Yet coal can be produced from both or from neither!

Thus capital and operational expenditure differ only in time and should be treated as the same as far as the tax system allows. Naturally the company will need to build into the analysis assumptions covering the following factors:

1 The market size and trends in the total market each year.
2 The market share which will be achieved each year.

1. *The Finance and Analysis of Capital Profits*, A. J. Merrett and A. Sykes, Longmans, 1963.
Capital Budgeting and Company Finance, A. J. Merrett and A. Sykes, Longmans, 1966.
2. *The Capital Budgeting Decision*, H. Bierman and S. Smidt, Macmillan, New York, 1960.
3. 'Risk and Return and D.C.F.', Balint G. Bodroghy, *The Director*, July 1966.

3 The translation of the above share into sterling sales and volume at a certain unit price.
4 Average discounts to the trade.
5 Transport costs.
6 Cost of goods on a running basis.
7 Extra cost of sales force and general overheads (it is argued in the chapter on pricing on page 136 that it is unrealistic to apportion full overheads to new products without taking the marginal profit factors into account).
8 Marketing expenditure, including trade bonuses, trade and consumer promotions, advertising, market research.

As a result the net profit position before tax should become evident on a running basis. Once the company adds on the capital costs of plant and allows for tax on the profits, for stocks and debtors and for investment benefits, the picture emerges of how much money comes in and goes out each year after tax. Of course each item should be in the correct time sequence so that tax payments should be debited to the years when they are actually paid and allowances credited to the years when the company actually receives them.

Finally an assumption needs to be made regarding the residual value of any assets involved at the end of the period evaluated. It is now possible to calculate and discount in comparison both with the company's criteria and with other projects competing for the company's limited resources.

Let us assume that there are two new products to be evaluated which, on best judgment, are estimated to have both a life of ten years and to have cash flows over the period as shown in the table overleaf.

It can be seen that the capital investment in Product A can be spread over the first two years and that the payout is relatively quick, i.e. the total investment has been recovered in the sixth year. The product begins to fall off then, however, and is almost dead by the eighth year.

Product B, on the other hand, requires the same capital expenditure of £200,000 but before the first year of marketing

	PRODUCT A		£'000	PRODUCT B		
	Outflow (payments	Inflow (receipts)	Net Cash Flow	Outflow	Inflow	Net Cash Flow
Initial outlay	100	—	(100)	200	—	(200)
Year 1	150		(150)	100	—	(100)
2	30		(30)	60		(60)
3		55	55	20		(20)
4		80	80		50	50
5		100	100		100	100
6		80	80		120	120
7		50	50		130	130
8		30	30		100	100
9		25	25		50	50
10		20	20		60*	60

* including residual value of £50,000.

and its losses initially are heavy, so that the investment is not recovered till the seventh year. It is thought, however, that Product B has better long-term potential than A and so its profits remain at a relatively high level until Year 10 when operating profits will drop sharply but when it is thought that it will still have assets commanding a considerable residual value. How should the company assess the projects on the D.C.F. system?

The simplest D.C.F. method is that which considers the net present value (N.P.V.) and the rate of return or yield of the project. It is usual to regard them as two alternative methods, but in fact they are very closely linked and both lead to the same results. Other D.C.F. methods exist which are more complicated and so probably not as useful in practice.

It must first be agreed that cash today is worth more than cash tomorrow, not for inflationary reasons but in real terms, because investment of available cash will lead to a greater amount in the future or alternatively because availability of cash reduces borrowing and so interest charges.

A public company should consider in calculating the minimum acceptable rate of return what its shareholders could earn on their investment themselves as well as interest costs to the company. Merrett and Sykes have shown that investors in equities have earned 6 per cent p.a. compound over the period 1919–1963 in real terms after tax, and estimate that we may expect a level of 7 per cent–8 per cent in the next few years.

This obliges the company to try to do at least as well and preferably better for its shareholders, so a minimum return of 9 per cent–10 per cent p.a. is by no means unreasonable, depending on the company's policy, the risk of the project, the markets in which the company is operating, etc.

If it is assumed that the company adopts the 10 per cent minimum, £110 in a year's time is only worth £100 this year, i.e. £100 next year are discounted by $\frac{100}{110}$ and so are only worth £91 this year. Similarly £100 in two years' time are worth only £86 now.

Discount tables at each rate of interest are readily available and if the company applies the 10 per cent discount to Products A and B the results would be as follows:

			£'000		
Year	A	B	Discount	Present Value at 10%	
	Cash Flow	Cash Flow	Factor	A	B
0	(100)	(200)	1·000	(100)	(200)
1	(150)	(100)	0·909	(136)	(91)
2	(30)	(60)	0·826	(25)	(50)
3	55	(20)	0·751	41	(15)
4	80	50	0·683	55	34
5	100	100	0·621	62	62
6	80	120	0·564	45	68
7	50	130	0·513	26	67
8	30	100	0·467	14	47
9	25	50	0·424	11	21
10	20	60	0·386	8	23
			Net Present Value =	1	−34

The Net Present Value should be equal to 0 if the project meets the discount criterion and this is almost exactly the case with Product A. Product B, on the other hand, clearly does not make the 10 per cent discount yield, as its high cash flows in the later years necessarily suffer high discounts, and in fact it can be calculated that it only provides 8 per cent return.

Thus the company has a clear picture of the financial viability of two products in relation to each other and to its set criteria. All the relevant factors are included in the calculation and it can even be argued that the uncertainty of estimating many years ahead is allowed for because of the heavy discount of the later years.

For example, an error of even 50 per cent in Year 10 would make relatively little difference to the projects.

At times, if two projects are compared, one may have a higher D.C.F. yield than the other and yet a lower N.P.V. when both are discounted at the same rates. This can happen when the first one is a smaller or shorter project even though its return is better. In such a case the company, having calculated that both projects meet the desired D.C.F. yield, could well choose the one with the lower rate of return but higher N.P.V. because it is a larger project in actual terms.

I believe that the D.C.F. method which I have tried to describe is simple and considerably ahead of other ways of evaluating the financial standing of a new product or of any investment for that matter. There is no reason why every company should not use this method on a continuous basis.

consideration of risk

However efficient the D.C.F. method is, it does not, of course, take away the risk in the underlying assumptions. As many as are possible and economic will be checked if the project progresses, but even so a large element of risk will remain.

For example, the cash flows for Products A and B could well have been different if a slightly altered view had been taken and it could happen that Product A could be logically shown to be an absolute disaster instead of returning a 10 per cent D.C.F. yield. Moreover, Product A could be more risky than Product B. What can be done to deal with these problems?

In general it is difficult to do more than employ some arbitrary methods to deal with risk. One is to require a higher return for risky projects. Another is to examine closely the factors involved in the cash flows and see what variations are possible. If the project has built into it a certain reserve so that if, say, only 75 per cent of the market share target is met the project is still not disastrous, then naturally the company feels safer in proceeding.

It is fairly common to allocate probabilities. For example, a company may face the following probabilities in percentage terms of achieving certain N.P.V. figures:

N.P.V. Below				
−£20,000	−£20,000–0	0–£20,000	£20,000–£40,000	Over £40,000
Product %	%	%	%	%
5	20	25	25	25
X Y —	5	80	10	5

The probabilities would be subjective, but nevertheless have some value if they result from a consensus of opinion through the executives working on the projects. In this particular case the company would need to decide whether to choose the safe Project Y or gamble with Project X with a 50 per cent chance of having an N.P.V. of over 20,000, but equally with a 25 per cent chance of a negative N.P.V.

An interesting approach to risk in relation to the rate of return has recently been described in the *Harvard Business Review*.[1] Plotkin and Conrad tried to see if there is in U.S. industry a correlation between the two factors, defining risk as the uncertainty in anticipating a certain outcome.

Risk was quantified by the dispersion in the return on capital of individual companies in an industry, a high dispersion signifying a high degree of risk and vice versa.

Study of 783 companies operating in 59 major Standard Industrial Classification (S.I.C.) fields of business over the period 1950–1965 showed in fact that a very close correlation between the dispersion factors and the return on capital does exist. Thus the highest variance in return on capital in the industries studied was in radio and T.V. broadcasting which also gave the highest return, whereas aluminium producers had the lowest variance and were very close to the lowest rate of return.

1. 'Risk/Return: U.S. Industry Pattern', G. R. Conrad and I. H. Plotkin, *Harvard Business Review*, March/April 1968.

This study is very encouraging as the concept is simple and practical. It seems worth while studying in a similar way the variance and the return on capital in various U.K. markets, so that the company would have a yardstick for selecting a certain rate of return corresponding with the amount of risk in a particular market.

eleven the name

what is there in a name?

When the time comes to discuss the name of a new product, even a well-organized and sophisticated company can go through the most extraordinary contortions to try and find one. Lists are compiled, subjective judgments are made, the chairman's and directors' wives are involved and finally, after a large amount of senior executive time has been spent on the matter, a name is finalized.

Yet how important is a brand name? Would Omo have fared better or worse if it had been named differently? Would Kenwood consumer durables have had a different fate if the company's founder had not been called Mr Ken Wood?

Although I have seen no factual evidence on this matter, it does not seem likely that the brand name plays an important part in the new product's success or failure. So many successful products have names which go against all the modern rules of name selection—they are difficult to pronounce, or can be confused with other names or have negative connotations—and yet continue to sell and to flourish.

For example, one would think that the confusion between Sunfresh and Suncrush must be against at least one of them and yet both are important brands of fruit squash. Volkswagen again do not seem to have suffered from what is a difficult name to roll off an English tongue, while fibres such as Terylene, Crimplene and Enkalon have become known despite their names.

The brand name seems, therefore, relatively unimportant

and certainly deserves less attention than is commonly given to it. So long as it does not arouse any strong negative reactions among its potential consumers, a name which is distinctive and easy to pronounce will be adequate for most products. What is far more important is the company's total naming policy in relation to both its existing and its new products.

The only exception is when the company tries to concentrate on the name, in the absence of any other physical or conceptual advantages over the competition, as the main selling point for the new product. For example, when Carreras launched Guards, the name seemed to represent the promotional platform and the company were able to exploit to the full the links with the Guards. Similarly, some new products have been particularly successful because of association with specific characters, e.g. the Batman Car in the toy market.

Clearly, in such cases as mentioned above, the name is the most important or one of the most important ingredients of the new product and so great care needs to be taken to ensure that it is suitable for the product, for the company launching it and for the market. These examples are very rare, however, occurring mainly in industries where it is impossible to achieve any product differentiation. If it is possible to do so, it is certainly advisable to aim for such differentiation rather than depend on the name alone—a tenuous reason for a new market entry.

company, range or brand names?

There are widely diverging views regarding the importance of the company name in relation to a range name and a brand name and often a company adopts different policies with different products.

A clear example of two opposite policies comes from the confectionery field if one compares Mars and Cadbury's. Mars obviously believe in individual branding and, apart from the Mars bar, its products have individual identities dissociated from the Mars name. Cadbury's, on the other hand, have used their name as an umbrella for a wide range of chocolate and sugar confectionery products and have continued this policy, though not always to the same extent, when diversifying into other food fields.

Another approach is provided by a company such as Brown and Polson, the U.K. subsidiary of Corn Products Incorporated, which uses the company name for some products, e.g. cornflour and blancmange, but uses the Knorr name for a range of its products and a brand name such as Mazola for an individual product.

The Mars approach has a number of advantages:

1 Each brand is given a clear identity with concentration of the promotional effort on the brand rather than on the company name.
2 If a brand does not succeed, or for some reason attracts an unfavourable reputation with the consumer, the other company brands do not suffer.
3 The company is able to market a number of directly competitive brands in the same market. The activities of Procter and Gamble and of Unilever in the detergent market are a good example of this.

The above advantages have serious corresponding disadvantages. The promotional concentration on each brand means that considerable expenditure is needed for each brand separately as there is no benefit from other consumer expenditure carried out by the company. There are, therefore, very few companies which can afford to carry out this policy.

Moreover, just as no other company brand can suffer if a particular brand fails, so success does not benefit any other brand either. It is a hazardous and lengthy business to develop a successful brand and to build it up to high sales and profit levels. It may seem unfortunate that, if this is achieved, the operation needs to be repeated for another brand from the same starting point without benefit from the previous success.

There are, therefore, definite advantages in marketing brands under the company name:

1 Every penny spent on promotion is used to increase the company franchise and so that of all its brands.
2 The cost is certainly lower than if the company uses the Mars approach.
3 There is a secondary public relations advantage. The public become conscious of the company's activities and so the company can benefit in many circumstances, e.g. if it has a public share flotation.
4 If the company obtains a favourable image, this must help any diversification into unfamiliar fields. For example, in its recent diversification efforts into various food fields, Cadbury's must have found their name to be one of their most important assets. Thus Cadbury's and McVities when they launched their cakes must have provoked the consumer reaction that here was a name they knew well for making good products, so it was worth trying the new product at least.

If Procter and Gamble, on the other hand, were to go into a new field, say into cooking oil which they market in the United States, from the consumer point of view they might as well be a new unknown company launching in Britain.

The use of range names is a useful compromise between the opposite Mars and Cadbury approaches. It enables a company to invest in a range name which will benefit a group of products rather than one brand only and so must be cheaper than the individual brand approach. It also gives the company more flexibility than it would have using the company name only, because it is easier to market product ranges which would not be suitable for the company name.

In general the large majority of companies would be well advised to market products under either their company name or range names. They cannot afford to do otherwise and to waste what is often their most important asset—a name or number of names known and respected by the consumer. It is noteworthy that recently (May, 1968) Jeyes announced that, following market research, they had decided to switch their policy of marketing individual brands such as Ibcol disinfectant and Sanilav lavatory cleaner to make use of the Jeyes name as a promotional umbrella.

If this argument is accepted, it follows that the company needs to know what its name or names mean to the consumer and whether they can be used for new products. Unless the company has such resources that it can disregard this point, its development and diversification policies will be seriously affected by the consumer relation to its names.

Moreover, once a company has such a name in its keeping, it is very valuable—often its most valuable asset—and great care needs to be taken to ensure that the name continues to be projected in front of the consumer and of the trade and that it is not devalued in any way. This means, of course, that the marketing policy on the company's existing products needs to take into account not only these products' needs but also the possibility of future new products being launched under the same name.

For example, Company Y had developed a range of successful consumer products after the war and by the late 1950's the brand name under which they were all marketed had achieved a very good image, implying high quality products justifying an above average price. In the last seven or eight years, however, the company decided to pursue a policy of aggressive price cutting and much of its marketing expenditure has been spent either on special bonuses to the trade or on consumer price-off promotions. In the short term, the results have been reasonable, but the implications for the long term are disastrous. The high quality name has now become associated with a bargain basement type of product which is never at a constant price, being always price cut. The results achieved during the 1950's in acquiring the high quality image have been dissipated and the company now finds it very difficult to use the brand name for new products. Either a new name needs to be found, with the resulting increase in promotional expenditure, or the policy on the existing brands needs to be reversed again to recover the lost image—a lengthy and again expensive process.

name and the consumer

Consumer research can be conducted to find out what the company names mean to the consumer. This is straightforward when related to the company's existing products, but it is not easy to establish what new products the names would be suitable for.

One solution is to face the consumer with an actual list of markets in which the company is interested and the results are often clear cut. For example, Raleigh, who have been recently trying to diversify from their bicycle business, would find it important to know whether their franchise is in products for boys, in wheeled products, in mechanical products, etc. Thus a food company such as Heinz, marketing mainly savoury products and a great exponent of the company name policy, may find it hard to market major sweet products or beverages, e.g. fruit squashes or night-time drinks, or upper-class products such as high-quality *hors d'oeuvres*.

It is, of course, possible to change the meaning of a name. It would be conceivable for Heinz to market eventually even non-food lines. It is clear, however, that the further the company moves from the present 'image' the more difficult the problem and the greater the expenditure needed to go into the new market.

name and the trade

From the trade's point of view a naming policy is much less important as the trade are well aware, of course, of manufacturers' activities in their markets, whatever the name given to each product.

It is well worth while, however, to explain carefully to the trade the company's naming policy, so that they can understand it and can also reflect it in their in store siting and merchandising activities.

name selection

The arguments already mentioned show that the important factor is the company's naming policy. Once this is established, if brand names are needed, as is usual, their selection should be a quick and simple process. Lists should be screened from the point of view of both registrability as well as suitability for the product and a short list should be included in consumer testing to cater for strong negative reactions. If it is shown that there are no negative reactions to a particular name, or number of names, the decision should be made quickly, so that attention can be given to some of the more real problems connected with the new product.

twelve the price

current practice

It is not even true to say now that every new product must have a price. Following the abolition of Resale Price Maintenance on most consumer products, the manufacturer can just decide on trade terms and let the retailer fix the price. Nevertheless, even if not governed by R.P.M., the majority of companies still fix the recommended price and, even if they do not, they must have a certain average retail price in mind when settling on trade terms. How is the retail price reached?

In practice not a great deal of thought is given to the retail price. Two factors are considered as the most important:

1 The net profit before tax after the costs of production, distribution and marketing have been accounted for together with an allocation of general and sales force overheads.
2 The retail selling price of products already in the market which are regarded as the nearest competitors to the new product.

If the competitive price can be equalled or bettered and there is an adequate profit margin, the company goes ahead and that is it. The price problem is solved.

Such an approach has the great virtue of simplicity and can work reasonably well. Whatever the economist or statistician has to say about pricing in terms of sophisticated pricing models, the marketer has neither the methods nor the time nor the money to measure intricate demand curves or other consumer response curves.[1]

At the same time to decide on the basis of what the costs happen to be and what other products cost without reference to any other factor ignores the importance of an important force in this decision—the ultimate consumer. How much is he or she ultimately prepared to pay?

The most modern procedure is to try to set the retail price which the market will bear, i.e. which enough consumers will be willing to pay to generate the most profitable short- and long-term sales volume for the product.

The long-term element needs to be introduced because, as Alfred Oxenfeldt[2] says, the question is not what is the most that the company can receive for the item quickly. Repeat purchasing as related to price is obviously important in most cases and so is possible reaction by other companies. For example, a high price accepted by the public may not be the most acceptable solution if it allows the entry into the market of a competitor at a lower price. Thus in this case the initial high price, however acceptable, could lead to a later decline in sales volume and in profits whereas a less greedy price at the outset may have served to block entry by new companies into the market.

A good example of a profitable policy based on low retail prices is provided by a small and private U.K. company which has dominated a particular food market in the U.K. for many years. The market grew substantially and attracted the attention of several large companies because of its potential and because they felt that the competition was relatively weak. Yet at least three companies found, after detailed market study and research, that the allegedly unsophisticated company was producing an excellent product in consumer terms and had kept its prices so low that they could do no more than offer product parity at much higher prices. The small company will

1. 'An Operational Approach to Product Pricing', Bill Darden, *Journal of Marketing*, April 1968.
2. *Pricing for Marketing Executives*, Alfred R. Oxenfeldt, Wadsworth Publishing Company Incorporated, July 1961.

probably never know how this low price policy—if it is a deliberate policy—has enabled it to keep the lion's share of a growing market and has prevented any effective competition.

At the same time, there are many examples of companies which have suffered by pitching their prices low and so found that in a competitive situation they were not able to raise them and had no room for an adequate margin to cover both marketing expenditure and profit.

The pricing policy needs certainly to be adapted to particular markets as there are considerable variations between markets in consumer price sensitivity. André Gabor and Clive Granger of Nottingham University[1] have done particularly useful work in comparing a number of markets in this area, but in general companies do not have enough reliable information on the degree of elasticity or inelasticity in consumer prices on the basis of which they can make pricing decisions.

Even so it is known that there are certain markets which can not only bear premium pricing, but may even favour it. For example, it is almost a marketing cliché that there have been cases when sales of certain cosmetic products have actually gone up following price increases. Consumer durables, e.g. cars, can also come in this category as the consumer buys not the car but the image.

Even in simple food markets, some brands have been very successful though priced considerably above the competition. The branding policy has been able to justify the extra price. In this context one needs to note particularly the role of advertising in the promotion of a selling concept which may not be based on any product advantage and yet is striking enough to warrant the high price. In fact the advertising and the resulting brand image become almost a product ingredient.

On the other hand, the consumer and specifically the housewife is much more price conscious than one would expect.

1. *Foundations of Market – Oriented Pricing: The Attitude of the Consumer to Prices: Symposium on Pricing:* Bradford University Management Centre, January 1967.

Even though research shows that she may not know what the actual price of a product is normally, if the price is cut by even 1d a significant sales increase often follows.

This price consciousness in grocery products has obviously been strengthened by the growth in the importance of self-service stores where the housewife has the continuous opportunity of seeing competitive prices side by side. This price consciousness is likely to increase and so companies will obviously need to take this factor into account when pricing new products.

The high degree of price consciousness on the part of the consumer is fully supported by the results of a study conducted by Gabor and Granger.[1] They covered only packaged household goods bought by the housewife—both food and non-food—representing fifteen different product categories. One would have expected that knowledge of prices would not have been particularly high as these products tend to have low unit prices, yet out of a total of nearly 5,300 purchases the housewives named a price in 82 per cent of the cases and of the prices which could be checked at the time about three quarters were within 10 per cent of the correct price. These seem astonishingly high results, but certainly confirm what many companies have found, i.e. that the British housewife is quite an expert regarding the price and quality of what she buys.

It is likely that, as a result of the high level of price consciousness on the part of the consumer, which will probably even increase in the future, the price that the market will bear will be based not on consumer ignorance but solely on the competitive advantage which the product will have over other products both in terms of product advantages and in terms of image. For example, the considerable advantage in convenience of frozen foods over conventional ones allowed the former to be launched in volume at a very much higher price and such a situation is likely to be repeated in the future.

1. 'On the Price Consciousness of Consumers', *Journal of the Royal Statistical Society*, Series C, Volume X No. 3, 1961.

Other types of high-priced products on the other hand, e.g. aerosol paints, have not provided the required degree of convenience over ordinary paints and so have only captured a very small market share. Again it is unrealistic to foresee that, in the circumstances, they will make substantial gains in the future.

There are obvious pricing problems if a company enters an existing market, but even if it can be wrong to try to match the competition their price serves as a useful reference. Yet, if these markets present pricing problems, what about the market which does not exist at all, so that there is no reference point?

In practice, the problem, if it is not to be treated completely subjectively, is extremely complex. At times a reference point can still be found by relating the entirely new product to the cost of products it may supersede or may be comparable to in the public eye. Thus the price of a hovercraft, though it is completely new, will need to be at least related to that of other forms of transport. A complete pie-kit product, e.g. Unilever's Promise, needs to be related to the cost on the one hand of buying ready-made pies and on the other to that of home baking. The first launderette should have had some reference to the cost of alternative methods of washing. It is in fact extremely rare that an innovation occurs which does not replace some current activities and so cannot be related to them in price.

Yet, even if reference points are found, how can one find out how much the market will bear? How much is a certain competitive advantage or a certain level of convenience worth in terms of price? These are questions which certainly need to be tackled.

pricing research

Despite the advances made in market research in recent years, even the most ardent practitioner will admit that there is still a long way to go before one can be satisfied with the market research in the field of pricing.

Ideally answers to such questions as 'Will you buy the product at 1s?' or 'How much more would you be willing to pay for this product than for what you normally buy?' should give an indication of the price for a new product and of the likely volume of sales at that price.

In practice, however, the problem lies in reconciling answers to such questions as the above with actual intention to purchase and with real purchasing rates. The consumer answers tend to be much too helpful as the consumer believes that the company wants to hear that he or she will buy from it in the future and the exaggeration factor can easily vary considerably according to the characteristics of each market.

A very common type of problem follows. If, say, one requires 5 per cent of all housewives to be regular buyers of the new product in order to meet the financial criteria set for the project and 15 per cent of a housewife sample say that they would be happy to buy the product regularly at the required price, is the research result good, bad or indifferent?

It may be possible to learn through asking such simple questions on every new product, so that comparisons between the research and the actual consumer purchasing behaviour can be made in cases when the products have gone on to be launched. Even so, such experience is unlikely to lead to quantitative weighting factors because of the differences between markets and because individual companies do not go on to launching such a high number of new products in any one type of product field that they can have a large enough base for any definite conclusions. Possibly, here is an area where everyone would benefit if a way could be found of aggregating all the research results belonging to a large number of companies to see whether general conclusions could be drawn.

At the moment, however, this kind of research at an early stage can only give very rough indications and a large amount of intuition or sheer guesswork is necessary in interpreting the results. The same applies to other research techniques connected with price, for example to the results of artificial price decision situations where the respondents are asked to take part in a lottery with prizes amounting to say £100 worth of certain products including the new product at certain prices and volume levels. A number of variations can be applied, but again one needs to guess at the relationship between choice in the artificial situation and that in the market place.

It follows that, in the early stages of a new product development project, the company can only obtain very broad indications regarding price and the relative importance of product advantages which could justify a higher price. On the basis of the research results and of intuitive interpretation one or more concepts are developed physically at certain prices and then research methods become more satisfactory if it is possible to measure actual sales in a number of stores at the point of sale.

In the case of packaged consumer goods, for example, there is no problem in taking a small number of outlets to be used as an experimental workshop. Comparison of sales at various price levels and possibly of different product concepts in relation to competitive products should lead to a relatively accurate assessment of the most profitable course of action and of the eventual profitability of the project.

In-store testing also has its disadvantages, needless to say, as there are control problems and in cases where a new concept needs explanation the product does not have the necessary advertising media support. In practice, however, promotions and explanations at the point of sale substitute for the media effect up to a point. Even if there is still some artificiality in the situation, it is nevertheless the nearest to real life before a full scale test market.

Consumer durables present a more difficult problem, as it is often impractical to produce only a small number. It follows, therefore, that the preliminary stages need to be much more thorough than with consumer goods and it is usual for both the trade and the consumer to be shown prototypes and asked reactions on the price.[1] It is also likely that, where the purchase is a really large one and so is of importance to the

1. 'Product Testing in the Automotive Industry', A. Leyshon, *Journal of the Market Research Society*, April 1968.

consumer, his reaction is likely to be more precise and trust-
worthy than in the case of a packaged product which may
represent a completely unimportant purchase.

Moreover the possibility of store testing of consumer durables should not be completely excluded. At times a product
very similar to what the company wants to introduce can be
found abroad and so it can be practical to import a number for
market research purposes, to be sold perhaps at various prices,
in a number of stores. Another possibility is that the company
could decide to have the product manufactured under contract by another company at first and so again, if the latter
already has facilities to produce products similar to what is
wanted, it may be possible to have a small number available
for store testing.

pricing decisions

Even if it is assumed that market research can give the company accurate information on which to make pricing decisions
—and, whatever the attitudes towards the research, assumptions on the relationship between price and sales volume need
to be made anyway—the process of decision on the pricing of
new products is by no means straightforward.

Some companies have rigid rules instructing them to ensure
that the new product is saddled with its rightful proportion of
overheads in the same way as existing products. This approach
does not take into account that the overheads already exist
and certainly penalizes the new product by forcing on it a price
which is higher than would be warranted on a marginal profit
basis.

Other companies have exactly the opposite outlook. They
believe that the importance of new products is such that the
existing products need to subsidize them and so no overheads
of any kind are charged to them at any rate in the first few
investment years. This approach can lead to unrealistically
low costing if the company is willing to shut its eyes to the new
product's overheads.

What is the answer? In my opinion the most useful approach in practice is well described in *Pricing for Profit and Growth* [1] where the authors argue rightly that it is a fallacy to consider that new products should be subject to full-costing and so should have a proper allocation of overheads on to them. What they should bear, however, is whatever it is estimated that they will add to the company's total current expenses, while they should not be charged with the actual development costs which must be allotted to the company's current operation in the development budget.

It may seem that these are details which will possibly change the price by only a minute amount. This is not so. They may not only affect the price but could also mean the difference between product failure and product success or between a decision to launch a product and one to kill it.

Let us look, for example, at hypothetical costings on a product which takes its 'rightful' share of overheads (Example A) as against the same product costed on extra total expenses it has led to (Example B):

	A	B
	d	d
R.S.P.	14·0	14·0
Trade margins	3·4	3·4
Transport	0·6	0·3
Net sales revenue	10·0	10·3
Cost of goods	7·0	7·0
Gross profit	3·0	3·3
Sales force	0·6	0·1
Other overheads	0·8	0·2
Marketing	1·0	1·0
Net profit before tax	0·6	2·0

Example A assumes trade margins with allowance for quantity discounts at 25 per cent of R.S.P., transport at 6 per cent, cost of goods at 70 per cent and fixed sales force and other overheads at 14 per cent of Net Sales Revenue. In practice these are realistic figures on the basis of a total overhead allocation and if one adds 10 per cent for marketing the resulting 6 per cent for net profit looks poor if it is assumed that the above costings

1. *Pricing for Profit and Growth,* A. Bergfeld, J. Earley, W. Knoblock, Prentice-Hall Incorporated, New Jersey, 1962.

relate to the time when the new product is on a running basis, having passed the investment period.

How different are the results in Example B! The same assumptions have been used except that the extra transport costs added by the new product to the existing transport costs are taken to be 3 per cent. Likewise extra sales force and other overheads are also assumed to be only 3 per cent of Net Sales Revenue. These seem reasonable assumptions if, as so often happens, the existing sales force is used for the new product and distribution is through current outlets.

The net profit in Example B is over 19 per cent of net sales revenue—a fine achievement. In my experience, a project would normally be rejected on the profitability forecast in Example A and progressed with great excitement on the basis of the costing in Example B.

Another way of looking at the difference between the two projects in terms of price is to calculate that, to achieve the profit of Example B with R.S.P. at 14d, the company would need to market the product at 16d if it insists on using the costing procedure as shown in A. Thus a 14 per cent price rise would be necessary to pay for the company's refusal to accept marginal costing and such a rise can be high enough to put the project out of court again.

If the principle of marginal costing for new products is accepted and assumptions can be made on the relationship between prices and sales levels, the price decision should be based on study of the consequences of every possible pricing decision.

The costs will be divided into:

1 Variable costs.
2 Fixed costs.

The variable costs will include the production costs for each unit of the product and the selling and distribution costs which will vary in direct relationship to the sales volume.

The fixed costs will include marketing expenditure, additional labour taken on to be engaged specifically in the operation and capital costs of the plant depreciated over its estimated economic life and allowing at the same time for obsolescence.

It follows that, within a certain volume bracket, the fixed costs will not change until, for example, the point has been reached where new overheads, such as the building of a new factory, are incurred.

Thus, if fixed costs are constant in the defined volume bracket, the price estimated to yield the highest gross contribution from the variable costs is the most profitable price for the new product.

If the example already used is applied here on the B costings divided into fixed and variable costs it is assumed that the breakdown would be as follows:

1.   *Variable Costs Per Unit*

	d.
Trade margins	3·4
Transport	0·3
Production	4·0
Sales force and other overheads	0·2
	7·9

2.   *Fixed Costs* — *at a volume of say 25 m. units*

Plant and additional product personnel	3·0
Sales force and other overheads	0·1
Marketing	1·0
	4·1

If the fixed costs are applied to a volume of 25 m. units, their total annual cost will be £427,000.

It is now possible to build up a table covering the estimated annual profitability during the economic life of the product and at different price levels. Let us assume that if the product is priced at between 12d and 19d, the resulting sales volume estimates will be shown as opposite.

Profitability Estimates at Different Prices

Price	12d	13d	14d	15d	16d	17d	18d	19d
Sales volume m. units	34	28	25	22	18	14	11	8
Gross contribution per unit before fixed costs (variable costs = 7·9d per unit)	4·1d	5·1d	6·1d	7·1d	8·1d	9·1d	10·1d	11·1d
Gross contribution before fixed costs £'000	582	595	636	652	607	531	463	370
Fixed costs £'000	427	427	427	427	427	427	427	427
Net profit before tax £'000	155	168	209	225	180	104	36	−57

On the basis of the above table 1s 3d per unit is the most profitable price. Even if the sales volume forecasts at different prices can only be very rough, it is felt that such an exercise as described here provides a useful basis for pricing and is not used by companies often enough.

Once the cost estimates are broken down into fixed and variable, the rest of the exercise is extremely simple.

thirteen market research for new products

need for normative data

Market research in various aspects plays an important part in the development of new products and is mentioned often throughout the book. Yet it is sad to reflect that one cannot really take advantage of all the research experience which has been collected over the years. Every day a number of new product surveys are being carried out and yet, when a company embarks on one, it needs to start from scratch as if none of the other companies' research had taken place.

Naturally an individual piece of research is confidential to the company for whom it has been done, but I take the research industry to task for not having established any procedure for aggregating results so that everyone can benefit from the general experience. The one exception is the Nielsen Company who show what can be done by studying the general conclusions arising from their retail audits and publishing the trends regularly in the *Nielsen Researcher* both in the U.S. and in the U.K. It is a shame that there are no signs of anyone trying to imitate them in this respect.

For example, study of a large number of surveys in many fields should lead to general conclusions showing certain relationships between different factors. It may be possible to relate preference in a blind product test to a subsequent market share; or the proportion of people saying they would buy a product to the number actually buying; or advertising awareness to consumer trial or shop distribution to knowledge of the product.

In some cases it may be impossible to draw any general conclusions and so the argument behind which we shield ourselves when asked about such general principles: 'it all depends' is right. I am convinced, however, that very important relationships can be established which would make marketing more scientific and so, hopefully, more profitable.

Until some central organization is set up to cope with the problem, the company must collect its own data bank. Even the biggest users of research will not be able to reach entirely satisfactory conclusions because the research is likely to have been confined to a narrow number of fields, but even so it is worth trying to study what information the company can collect from its files. It can be very much better than nothing and yet very few companies seem to think such an approach worth while.

For example, a middle-sized consumer goods company, operating in a number of markets linked with each other, recently collected all the data it had from just six test markets in its product field. Consumer research and retail audits had been conducted in each case, so it was possible to see if there was any relationship between the weight of marketing expenditure, the levels of brand awareness, consumer trial and consumer sales. Interestingly, even the very modest number of six test markets produced a general pattern which proved invaluable when another test market was planned in a similar product field.

In the same way most medium-sized and large companies have a mass of past market research data in their files. However rough and difficult to compare, it can still provide useful guidance to those planning more research on new products.

Perhaps the day will come when we shall all know on the basis of 40,000 surveys that a new product achieving a 60:40 preference over the brand leader in a blind product test has a 75 per cent chance of obtaining at least half the brand leader's sales in the first year of marketing. Until that happy day comes—and I doubt that it ever will—companies must seek their normative data as well as they can. Such past research is worth its weight in gold.

use of research

I am sorry if I also sound a critical note against the way in which market research is often used in new product development, but I feel that all too frequently it is conducted for its own sake and not with the company's profits in mind. For example, if a company is interested in a specific product field, it is too easy to decide that it is necessary to know immediately everything about it. A mammoth operation is mounted to check on consumer usage and attitudes, volumes of tables are produced and over £5,000 can easily be spent. A company needs only to be mildly interested in twenty markets to spend £100,000 or more on very broad and not particularly helpful research.

There is a danger of spending too much on market research in development, just as it is dangerous to spend too little. It may seem a cliché, but the justification of a piece of research should be in terms of the financial return likely to be derived from it and compared with the decisions which would need to be taken without market research information.

I am a strong supporter, therefore, of regarding the use of market research in the development process as a bit by bit operation, on the same principles as the step by step development process of a new product which has been already described.

Thus instead of the proverbial £5,000–£10,000 large survey at the start of the operation, it seems far more beneficial to start off by collecting all the desk research which may include published market research data. A small piece of research costing only £300–£500 could follow to give the company a feel of the market, even if it can be hardly quantified on the basis of such research. If the project is still viable, it may then be advisable to find out further information on one specific aspect, following the previous research, and say £500–£1,000 could be spent at this stage. Again the project could re-evaluated and, if it passes the test, further research may be necessary costing now, perhaps, £1,000–£2,500.

Altogether it is possible that the company finishes up by spending more by adopting the type of system described above than if it had undertaken one large survey at the beginning. This assumes, however, that the project progresses through the various stages to justify all the pieces of research one after another. In practice a number of projects will be eliminated early, so the limitation of research expenditure at the beginning should lead to savings.

Secondly, in a multi-stage research operation the company learns from one stage to the next, so the research incorporates the lessons arising from the preceding work and answers the specific questions raised by the previous research. The final results therefore should be much more useful than those of a single survey at the outset of the operation.

Moreover, there is general reluctance to use crude forms of fact finding, if the finances of a project do not warrant anything else at that stage. For example, telephone research or postal research may not be ideal and certainly good arguments can be advanced against them. They should not be spurned, however, as if research technique were some sacrosanct factor in the development process.

For example, a small number of questions among upper and middle class women could easily be asked by telephone of telephone-owning housewives. Or reactions towards a consumer durable can be obtained by means of a postal questionnaire among past buyers of the product. In such cases, where the respondent is interested in the subject, response rates of even 80 per cent have been recorded in postal surveys.

So let us not scorn research methods which at times may seem cheap and nasty. Even such pieces of research have a role to play in new product development.

concept research

In theory it appears possible to conduct a market survey into a market to discover consumer characteristics and attitudes and to find gaps in the market which can lead to a suitable product concept. In practice, however, it has already been mentioned that such an approach tends to be not very fruitful, simply because the public find it difficult or impossible in most markets to express any desire for new products.

Similarly, the problem exists in a group discussion, although it is then possible for an experienced discussion leader to direct the conversation into specific areas. In general the consumer thinks very narrowly about a market and the products in it. His or her terms of reference are naturally the existing products which are usually satisfactory and any suggestions for new products tend to be extremely close to the existing one.

The experience mentioned above refers particularly to fast-moving packaged goods. In consumer durables where an item costs a considerable amount of money and purchase follows careful evaluation by the consumer, it is likely that knowledge of existing products can be high and so suggestions for product improvements and completely new innovations could result.

It is noteworthy that Massey Ferguson claims to start its process of new product developmnet with market research.[1] Similarly continuous consumer attitude studies in cars, T.V. sets, washing machines, etc. among buyers of both the company's and the competitor's products could well be fruitful. It is important, however, for the company to be happy that the consumers are really interested and knowledgeable enough to talk usefully about a product field, if such research is to be undertaken.

Unless, therefore, there are likely to be very clear cut consumer suggestions for new products, it is better for them to come from the company as a result of internal concept search methods. Then it is most fruitful to ask the consumer for reactions towards the suggested concepts.

Even so the concepts, unless extremely simple, are not easy to grasp in an abstract form and it is advisable to be able to show a physical representation in the form of a product or a

1. Address to P.E.R.A.: L. A. Parker, Marketing Director, Massey Ferguson, June 1968.

rough prototype or even in the form of an illustration, possibly as part of an advertisement.

Once there is something concrete which can be shown to the consumer, which requires comment on an idea rather than a long leap into the unknown, he is often extremely helpful in reacting either in individual depth interviews or in group discussions. It is certainly possible to go some way to validation of concept through the use of such methods, although what cannot be done with any precision is to quantify the importance of the concept and so find out how much the consumer is willing to pay for it in practice. This can only be found in a market place situation.

product testing

Little advance seems to have taken place in product testing since at least the middle 1950's. Basically, where possible a product is given to the consumer 'blind' i.e. unidentified, to be compared with a popular competitive product already on the market, which of course is also tested blind. If the new product wins or at any rate shows no strong negatives, then it can be assumed that it is worth while going on to the next stage. In the case of durables it is necessary to use prototypes from which reactions are obtained.

In practice, product research, though it sounds simple, raises certain problems which can be listed as follows:

1 What factors should be included in the comparison between the two products and what importance should be given to each one? The consumer may prefer one product on certain grounds and the other on others and it is also possible that the most important points of distinction between the two products, as far as the consumer is concerned, are not listed at all in the questionnaire.

It is useful, therefore, to predetermine, whether from research information or on judgments, the most important consumer factors in the particular market and their relative importance. On this basis, and subject to any changes arising from the actual concept of the new product, it should be possible to include the important factors, while knowledge of their relative importance would be vital at the interpretative stage.

2 The results of a quick test can be very different from what would happen in practice over a considerable time span. For example, a company testing a new snack product against an established one found that the former had good comparative acceptance when a small portion of both products was eaten. The project went on to a test market, but there it was found that the test results had been misleading because the new product, though palatable in small doses, palled when eaten in large quantities and over a longer period. Similarly it is well known that in a small product test Acid Spangles were the most popular variety because of their strong flavour, but over a period more neutral varieties would in fact sell much better because Acid Spangles can be eaten in small doses, but not in large quantities.

If it is suspected that this problem could arise, it is important to give the consumer a large quantity of the product or to repeat the test a number of times at close intervals.

3 Absence of strong negatives does not reflect any positive feelings. It is possible for a product to arouse little or no unfavourable comment, but later the product can still perform badly in the market place, if it does not offer any strong positive advantage.

Interpretation of the product testing can be a problem. It is also possible that the new product, although well behind the competitor overall, scores particularly well with a segment of the sample, so that narrow appeal to a sector of the market could be a possibility.

For this reason it is useful, when market segmentation is a possibility, to use a much bigger sample than is usual for product testing, in order to see whether preference for the new product is strong in a particular subsample, even if it is weak overall.

Despite the problems in the product testing of consumer goods, the risks are still not too great because the company can go on to later stages such as tests in a number of shops or in a test town or a larger area to obtain further indications of consumer reaction. In the case of consumer durables this is often not possible, so the product testing stage is much more crucial, being nearer to the eventual final steps in the decision process regarding the product.

At the same time, it is very rare for a completely new concept to be introduced in durables, as a manufacturer normally has as a useful starting point a wealth of data on consumer reactions towards existing products. For example, a car manufacturer[1] faced with continuous need to introduce new models could well conduct continuous research on attitudes towards their cars among car owners—Mr. Leyshon mentions a company conducting three monthly surveys—to build up a background against which to introduce new models.

Naturally, it is again crucial to establish the relative importance of each factor and it is not easy to realize that in a product with a high engineering and design content the consumer could be particularly influenced by the door locks of a car or the knobs on the door handles of furniture.

Because of its great importance in the development process, the product testing of durables is itself protracted over a number of stages as the product becomes developed. Thus, in the case of a car, consumer attitudes could first be sought towards an illustration, then a clay model mock up, then possibly a fibre-glass model and finally a sheet-metal one, the reactions to each step enabling the company to revise the model and test it at the next stage.

Timing is naturally an important factor in the development of a new durable, the gestation period of a new durable being longer than that of an elephant. Leyshon quotes four years for

1. 'Product Testing in the Automotive Industry', A. L. Leyshon, *Journal of the Market Research Socity*, April 1968.

a car as an average period from the initial sketches to the production model and the product research could well be
stretched out over most of that time.

other forms of research

Other types of research are used, as already mentioned, in the
development process, to assist in the naming, pricing, packaging, advertising, test marketing, etc. More details are to be
found under the appropriate chapters.

fourteen the trade

reaction to new products

There is an attitude among certain companies, particularly
the larger ones and those heavily oriented towards the consumer, that the trade are not particularly important in the
new product development process. If the product seems to
meet the company criteria in the planning stages and if it has
a consumer advantage over the competition, then surely the
trade will be no problem. They will simply funnel the product
from the company to the consumer and this will in the process
benefit them as well.

This reasoning may be plausible, in theory, but does not
always work in practice, because the trade have become an
increasingly important factor. Whereas even in the early 1960's
any well known company launching a new product could
guarantee a sterling distribution level of, say, 60 per cent in
grocers and up to 90 per cent in chemists, the situation has
since become much more difficult. By 1968 the same company
would be delighted with 40 per cent–45 per cent in grocery
outlets.

The concentration of power among the trade into fewer and
larger groups and the consequent general increase in scientific
methods in retailing has led to a notable decline in stock levels
and particularly in the number of brands stocked. For example
a chain of multiple grocers, who at one time would have
stocked six or seven brands in a market of any size, now tend
to stock the brand leader, their own label and possibly one
other brand as an alternative. To persuade the retailer to add

to those three needs either an extremely attractive and so unprofitable offer or a product with such superiority over the competition that the sceptical buyer will accept it on that basis alone.

N. H. Borden Jr[1] shows in his U.S. study how buying committees reacted to a salesman's presentation of a new product introduction. In many cases the haphazard nature of the decision whether to stock it or not was astonishing. Decisions were made very quickly—one in thirty seconds—there were no specific buying criteria and only in one case among the many quoted was any consideration given to the effect on inventory. Even so only a minute proportion of new products were accepted in the U.S. supermarkets at that time.

It is likely that buying decisions have recently become more scientific both in the United States and in Britain, even if there is doubtless a proportion of buyers in buying committees who are behaving very amateurishly. However the buyer behaves, the odds must be against the new product, on the one hand because of conservatism and on the other on the basis of financial reasoning, e.g. to cut down stocks.

It is important, therefore, and it is becoming increasingly so, that the company should consider carefully the likely reaction of the trade to a new product launch and should prepare its presentation to the trade meticulously. It pays.

variation in trade attitudes

The trade by themselves can make or break a new product and yet this point is not always appreciated when one attempts to make the invariably difficult analysis of reasons why some products fail and others succeed. It also seems that the trade have different attitudes to different companies which have an important bearing on the trade attitudes to new products.

There are some companies, for example, which are particu-

1. *The Introduction of New Products to Supermarkets,* Doctoral Thesis, Harvard Business School, N. H. Borden Jr, December 1964.

larly unpopular with the trade who are nevertheless forced to stock existing brands. Yet it is much easier to find reason against accepting their new products if possible, whereas sympathy is extended at times to small companies. This could explain why there have been surprising examples of successful new products launched by small companies competing with much larger ones.

It also seems that the trade regard companies in a certain context and so look on their new products with favour if they are in some fields but not in others. For example, two large companies recently launched similar toiletry ranges in the same area. One achieved immediately very high distribution, while the other found it almost impossible to have any at all, the main difference being that the latter was not regarded by the trade as a toiletry company. Similarly another recently launched a product that has been most successful for only one reason. It was exactly the same product as that of the brand leader, but the latter was very unpopular with the trade who, for once, welcomed the 'me-too' product with open arms. On the other hand, another recent new product was victimized by some buyers because it was a food product produced by the subsidiary of a chemical company and the buyers felt strongly that food and chemicals should not go together!

If it is accepted that the trade are vital in a new product launch and that they will react to a new product in different ways, according to their views of the company marketing it, it follows that each company must not only cultivate the trade but must also find out whether the trade regard them as particularly suitable to market products in some markets and not in others. Such trade enquiries prove normally to be extremely useful. Even if the company may still decide that it has such a good proposition that it will persuade the trade to accept a product from them in what seems an unsuitable product field, nevertheless it is important to assess beforehand the level of acceptance or of resistance which is likely to be offered.

marketing support

The need to have an important product advantage has already been mentioned, so that the trade should have good justification for stocking.

Another particularly important factor is the marketing support which the new product will be given. In fact in Neil Borden Jr's enquiry in the United States it was apparent that the product by itself was not considered particularly important by the trade. More important was the marketing programme supporting it and, at least in some cases, the buying committee accepted a product solely because of the marketing support. I had a similar experience when selling a new product to chemist wholesalers in the U.K. Before I could describe the product, I was asked whether it was going to be on television and, when they heard that it would be, the buyers immediately expressed interest without even knowing what the product was!

At the same time there can be a difference between promise and performance. Naturally a company must put its marketing programme in the most favourable light, but even so many companies have done themselves a disservice through ridiculous exaggeration.

For example, if a company intends to spend on advertising, say, £30,000 over three months in an area representing 25 per cent of the country, there is a strong temptation to calculate the equivalent national expenditure over twelve months and to announce a very strong advertising campaign of £500,000 without being too particular about explaining this figure. And this is the kind of a temptation to which some well-known companies have succumbed in the past.

Similarly, even a casual examination of advertisements in trade publications will show extraordinary promises. They claim that hundreds of millions of people will be reached by the campaign, presumably multiplying actual coverage by the estimated frequency of this coverage. Or hundreds and even thousands of television spots are mentioned, so that if there are 50 spots in each of 8 areas the spurious total becomes 400 spots! It is also by no means unknown for promised campaigns to disintegrate mysteriously after a few weeks, although of course a company has every right and indeed a duty to its shareholders to cut expenditure which is proving unprofitable.

It is not surprising, therefore, that the trade are sceptical of such promises of support, particularly if they have been caught out a number of times. So even if a company benefits once or twice by persuading the trade to stock and display a new product to a degree which is completely out of proportion with the product potential and its marketing programme, in the long term the company's approach must rebound against it. It must be expected, therefore, that some companies who always match promise with performance have established better trade relations than others who appear to have let the trade down at times. Companies would do well to appreciate this factor, as many have done already.

It is also worth noting the type of marketing support which the trade appreciate particularly. As far as advertising is concerned, every survey published on the subject shows that in the case of product groups for which television is applicable a dominant majority of the trade believe it to be more effective than other media. This attitude has been confirmed whenever I have had an opportunity of talking to the trade on this subject.

The trade attitude does not mean, of course, that television must be used for every new product, but the trade factor should at any rate be considered when the advertising media are chosen. Moreover it is sometimes advisable to devote part of the budget to co-operative advertising with the trade. This works particularly well if the trade consists of a small number of outlets where support is particularly important, e.g. in the case of a new motor car or of a new type of holiday. In both markets the local outlet—garage or travel agent—has a considerable influence on the customer in an advisory capacity, so a close link in the promotion between retailer and manufacturer is likely to be beneficial. There is also a trend in packaged goods towards exclusive promotions with the large and increasingly powerful multiple chains and again these could be used for new products, especially in order to obtain distribution in the chain concerned.

The economics of below-the-line expenditure, i.e. trade and consumer promotions, need in fact to be considered carefully in the launch of a new product. Their growing importance in most markets coupled with the prevalent abolition of resale price maintenance has led to a considerable amount of pressure by the trade on manufacturers. The amount devoted to trade margins and special discounts has been growing generally and in some cases, particularly in certain packaged goods markets, the manufacturers have found themselves in a very difficult position. Finding perhaps that a trade bonus led to a sales increase, a company would repeat it. The competition would then follow with a higher bonus and over the years the market would become one dominated by trade bonuses, hardly any product being sold to the trade at its full price. Thus there are companies with sales forces which believe that they cannot sell without very heavy trade bonuses, so that there are expenditures of even £500,000 on trade promotion and only £100,000 on consumer advertising. Such circumstances have also led to very strong pressure on manufacturers' margins and some companies have even become bankrupt directly because of this reason.

It is not easy for a company to break away from the pressure on trade discounts for its existing products, once it has opened the door in this way. It is possible, however, to change the situation as far as new products are concerned by taking a strong position from the beginning, and companies have found in fact that they have been able to maintain their trade prices on new products even though they continue to give away part of their margins on the established ones.

Thus the company must reconcile its desire for good trade relations with the need for a strong attitude on trade discounts. In practice this is not as difficult a problem as it may appear at first. Refusal to limit trade discounts is a sign of strength and would even lead to more respect by the trade towards the particular company.

This does not mean that trade discounts can be eliminated completely for a new product. They are the established method for obtaining initial distribution and should certainly be used in the first journey cycle, as long as it is made very clear to the trade that the first journey is a special occasion and that the discount will not be repeated. On the subsequent calls the sales force must in fact resist the temptation of giving further discounts and instead the company should concentrate on consumer promotion in the form of advertising, sampling, couponing, competitions and any other method of stimulating consumer demand. A strong sales force should be able to persuade the trade that it is in the interest of the latter as well as of the company to concentrate all expenditure to persuade the consumer to buy from the retail outlet.

The marketing plans for the new product should provide, therefore, for a strong pricing policy and for the bulk of the expenditure to be devoted to stimulation of consumer demand.

presentation to the trade

As a few buyers are now so important in a new product introduction, it follows that much attention needs to be given to the method whereby the company presents the new product to these buyers. This means not only the proverbial launching party, but also the occasion when the company faces the buyer and needs to persuade him to stock and promote the new product.

There has already been a trend in some companies to form a small sales force of senior sales executives to look after the large buyers only. In many cases it is also likely to be profitable to build up a detailed presentation for these buyers. After all, if the company has gone through the development process up to test market or a launch, the evidence of the opportunity in the market and the suitability of the product to exploit this opportunity should be as relevant to the trade as it is to the company. If the company had not thought that there would be good reasons for the trade to accept the product, they would not have gone ahead.

There are also accounts when an individually prepared presentation could be justified despite the high cost which this would usually entail. There is a moral in the story of one company launching a new product, which prepared a very elaborate presentation to be used specifically for one account. After the presentation, the company's managing director exploded when he saw the bill for its preparation and threatened to refuse to authorize payment. When, however, news came through of the order received as a result of the presentation, the managing director immediately forgot his threats. It had been well worth the expense.

There must be many such cases when an elaborate presentation, possibly incorporating exclusive promotional deals for a large buyer, will justify the effort and expenditure involved.

importance of company to the trade

A company's importance to the trade depends largely on two factors:

1 Its size.
2 Its range of products.

As competition grows, so the size of a company becomes increasingly important in dealing with the trade. A large company with a wide spread of products should be in a stronger negotiating position, other things being equal, than a small company in the same field. In fact as the trade are bound to continue their policy of stock rationalization, it must follow that it is the small company's products which will tend to be cut out, unless there are specific reasons for not doing so, while the large company's products will take over.

It follows that companies, if they want to survive, will need to include in their planning provision to grow to the required size to make them important to their particular trade buyers.

Some mergers can only be explained if the main purpose was growth to a unit of a certain size rather than short-term profits.

Similarly, the company needs to consider the importance to the trade of the product range it offers. Even large international companies can have built up their turnover on peripheral products and they are likely to be vulnerable in the long term against competitors who also market more essential very high volume products which must be stocked by the trade.

A number of companies have already realized how vital it will become in the future to have in their range products which will be important enough to the trade to maintain distribution for the other products too. In fact the addition to the existing company range of one or more products which will open the door for their sales force as 'lead lines' can easily be one of the objectives in the company's development policy. For example, an international company made a very large acquisition in the U.K. which has been much criticized for being unprofitable in the short term. The main objective of the acquisition, however, was to add to the company's power in the long term and the combination of the two companies will have an important range of products and considerable negotiating strength in the future. On the basis of these criteria the acquisition has been a great success.

fifteen marketing expenditure

need for brand promotion

New consumer product launches are normally accompanied by large expenditure on marketing and one wonders at times whether this is always justified. Would it perhaps be more profitable for the company to let the product, if good enough, speak for itself? I know that such thoughts are anathema to the modern marketing approach, but hang the theoretical approach if there is more profit elsewhere.

In fact in most cases a company does need to spend on marketing and particularly on brand promotion for two main reasons:

1 To establish an identity for the new product which will help it both against existing products and against future competitors.
2 To fight the 'own brands'.

The first point is obvious and naturally important. At the same time a company could launch a new product very cheaply by producing it for a retail organization rather than marketing it by itself. Such a policy could be attractive in the short term or for a small company without resources for branded marketing, but which at the same time desires to retain its independence.

Such a policy would be indeed shortsighted, however. Own brands have increased in importance in recent years, especially in packaged goods where in many cases they represent up to 20 per cent–25 per cent of the total market, and it is likely that they will continue to expand if the U.S. experience is to be repeated.

Own brand business represents useful marginal profit for the large consumer goods manufacturers, but it also provides a very important reason for launching branded products as well. Only the latter provide any security for the company by forcing the trade to stock them if they establish a consumer franchise which the own brands cannot satisfy.

expenditure levels

Once the company accepts the need for marketing expenditure to support a new product launch, it is necessary to decide the level of this expenditure. Yet, however extraordinary it may appear, there is not any accepted way of deciding this level. There seems to be no method which can even begin to claim that it is scientific despite the frequency with which such decisions need to be made by so many companies.

A study recently completed by the Marketing Society[1] reviewed current methods of setting advertising and marketing appropriations, and serious objections were raised in all cases.

Basically three main factors need to be considered in this connection:

1 The market type.
2 The required market share.
3 The competition.

If the market is ripe for considerable expansion, the current expenditure need not be considered too closely as the company will probably want to spend at a much higher rate to capture the lion's share of the expanded market. If, on the other hand, the aim is to enter a developed market and to obtain volume for the new product at the expense of the companies in the market rather than from market expansion, then very close attention will certainly need to be paid to what is happening in the market currently.

1. Setting Advertising Appropriations, 1967.

The degree of brand loyalty in the market will obviously affect the level of the appropriation. There are some markets, e.g. shampoos and other hair products such as hairsprays or colourants, which thrive on variety as the consumer is always anxious to try a new product. By contrast there are other markets, e.g. bread, where the consumer is extremely conservative and so there are very few new product introductions.

It follows, therefore, that the marketing effort in a fickle market needs to be relatively smaller at the outset than in a conservative one and the expenditure will need to be concentrated on the stages after the launch to ensure that initial consumer trial is translated into the required rate of repeat and regular purchasing. The conservative markets, on the other hand, will tend to require a very high level of expenditure just to break into the market and obtain consumer trial. If this is achieved the follow-up stages leading to regular purchasing probably require less effort and expenditure than in the fickle markets.

Even after the company has established clearly the characteristics of the market which it intends to enter, the relationship between market share and marketing expenditure still needs to be calculated and informed guesswork or 'intuition' is the main basis for decision. Nielsen[1] have analysed new products in packaged goods and have concluded, on the basis of detailed study of such new products, that on average a new product in its first two years needed to spend on advertising at twice the rate of the established competition in the product field. Thus, in order to obtain a market share of 10 per cent in a developed market, the new product would need to have 20 per cent of the marketing expenditure.

As a rule of thumb such a ratio is reasonable because in most cases the new product must spend at a rate considerably higher than the average in the market in order to be noticed and to break through as well as to combat the marketing effort which the established companies have accumulated over the years. Thus a new entrant into, say, domestic appliances would

1. *Nielsen Researcher*, January/February 1964.

need normally to spend extremely heavily to compensate for the millions of pounds which have made names such as Hoover and Hotpoint well known and respected by both the trade and the public.

At the same time, it must be noted that in the Nielsen study there are large variations around the average and that some successful new products were introduced at no more than the average rate in the market. The quality of the marketing effort and the degree to which the new product has clear advantages over the existing ones are both factors which need to be taken into account.

One recent new product succeeded despite very modest support whereas another introduction in the same market by a very large company backed by expenditure at five times the rate of the former product was a complete failure. The main difference was in the quality of the marketing, the smaller expenditure being used unquestionably much more effectively than the large one.

If the product has very strong advantages over the competition, it is possible to spend relatively little just to demonstrate the advantages so long as there is no need to pre-empt possible competition for the advanced product. Thus Turtle Wax quickly established itself as a leading car polish with relatively little marketing expenditure. Similarly Wilkinson Sword obtained a large share of the razor blade market with their stainless blade again with fairly small marketing expenditure which later needed to be raised very considerably because of competition from Gillette.

It is useful also to attack the expenditure problem from the other end, i.e. to decide what needs to be done and then consider how much is necessary to do it. In this way one will avoid the danger of reaching an expenditure level which makes sense in relation to the market and the competition, but none at all in absolute terms. For example, a company intending to enter a market of £4m. at R.S.P. in which total marketing expenditure is £250,000 may conclude quite reasonably that it should obtain an average share of 10 per cent in the first two years by spending no more than £60,000–£70,000 p.a. Yet if demonstration is an important part of the promotional plan so that television is necessary, then £60,000–£70,000 is completely unrealistic for a national television campaign. The sum is wrong in absolute terms.

Possibly a solution is to interrelate the various factors affecting the marketing expenditure by quantifying them on the basis of assumptions even if these are subjective. Let us assume a market of £10 m. which is not thought capable of much expansion, and which is traditionally conservative. The company believes it has found a product with an important advantage over the competition who spend in total about £900,000 p.a. and are estimated to be willing to increase this to some £1.2 m. if a new entrant comes into the field. The new product lends itself to demonstration, so television would be most useful as an advertising medium in this case.

The company believe that they can obtain up to 15 per cent of the market in the first year with a considerable marketing effort, but how much should they spend? If the Nielsen ratio is applied, so that the company will need to spend at twice the average rate, the company will need to spend about £500,000, i.e. 30 per cent of £1.7 m. which is the forecast of the total marketing expenditure in the market. Let us now apply the various weighting factors. The product advantage is considered very considerable—enough to justify a reduction of 25 per cent in the expenditure. The competition although established consists of sleepy companies who are unlikely to provide vigorous opposition, so a further discount factor of 5 per cent can be added. On the other hand the market has shown itself to be conservative and a real effort will be needed to induce the consumer to try the new product, so 10 per cent weighting is added on that score. Thus after the weighting factors are considered the expenditure comes down by 20 per cent to £400,000.

At the same time, the company needs to consider what level is necessary to make the required impact. The television campaign needs to be fairly strong nationally, so a sum of £250,000 would be by no means exaggerated for this purpose. About £100,000 will be necessary for a strong programme of below the line activity, including initial trade bonus, consumer promotions, and point of sale material. If some £20,000 is added for research the total comes to £370,000.

Against the above calculation a budget of £400,000 is very reasonable, and allows a reserve for flexible use during the first year. So, if £400,000 for the first year leads to the required profits on the project when incorporated in the profit and loss calculations, it can be adopted as the figure to be assessed further at the test market stage. Possibly the effects of £400,000 on marketing expenditure can be measured in the test market in comparison with another expenditure level in another area.

I am sorry if the reader is scandalized by such a haphazard approach to the establishment of an expenditure level which is often high and always important to the company. It is hoped that in time this will change and that there will be a wealth of data which can be used to decide on the right level of the marketing budget. At the moment, however, despite the claims of operational research and of simulation exercises, the marketing expenditure level for a new product is still a matter of personal judgment and intuition.

the pay-off period

The marketing expenditure for a new product is very much affected by the company's investment policy. This governs the number of years which the company is prepared to wait before beginning to make profit and then recovering its investment.

When companies were production-oriented, profits were usually considered on a short-term basis only. If a new product was not judged to contribute to the company's profits very quickly the project was shelved.

As companies became more aware of marketing considerations in the 1950's, the importance of long-term investment began to be appreciated. In fact it was generally recognized that it was not possible to launch a new product in a competitive market without a long-term investment policy allowing for a very strong and unprofitable launch to establish the product to a level at which the expenditure can be allowed to fall and a profitable position is reached. Thus pay-off plans lasting even five, six or seven years were thought acceptable for consumer goods and various new products were launched which represented a heavy burden on their companies' short-term profits.

Moreover they provided a serious problem in forecasting because what the company saw in the first year or two of national marketing and what could be verified in test market was a huge loss at a certain level of marketing expenditure. In theory the situation would change later, but just because the unprofitable forecasts were realized in practice there was no reason to have faith that the later forecasts of a change to a profitable position would follow. In fact a number of companies found that they could not diminish their marketing effort as planned because of the competitive position in the market and yet had gone so far that they did not want to abandon the project.

For example, a company could have been satisfied with the following investment plan:

Year	1	2	3	4	5
Market share	5%	8%	10%	12%	13%
Marketing expenditure £'000	250	200	150	150	150
Net profit before tax £'000	—80	—10	+50	+90	+110
Cumulative profit	—80	—90	—40	+50	+160

In theory, it is reasonable to assume a rise in share from 5 per cent to 13 per cent in the fifth year and, after allowing for all the items of expenditure, a profit picture would result whereby the product would begin to run at a profit in the third year and cumulatively in the fourth, so long as marketing expenditure fell from £250,000 in the first year to £150,000 in years, 3, 4, and 5.

Yet if the company goes into a test market and obtains 5 per cent share with expenditure equivalent to £250,000, is this a good result? It fits in with the plan above, but the result does not provide the slightest reassurance that the share will go up to 13 per cent and that expenditure will drop to £150,000 by the fifth year. And these are crucial assumptions. If one or the other does not occur, the project is a disaster!

In the last two or three years, therefore, attitude towards long-term investment projects has changed. It is now recognized that there are a number of factors against long-term investment, the main ones being as follows:

1 The rate of change in the environment and in technology is certainly increasing, so a product designed to satisfy specific consumer needs will surely die if these needs suddenly disappear or are radically changed.

2 In the very competitive situation which exists in most markets the lead achieved by any new product is very short-lived before it is copied by the competition. It is not surprising, therefore, that although old-established brands are often very vigorous and even growing after 50–60 years, the life of a new product is very short indeed.

3 There is little evidence that long-term investment policies have been particularly successful.

There is a move, therefore, towards a compromise between the old production-oriented and the new marketing-oriented attitude to investment. The advantages of launching at an initially unprofitable rate in order to make the necessary impact on the consumer and the trade are still recognized, but there is reluctance to wait too long for the pay-off.

I am convinced that the latest attitudes are correct, because companies moved much too far into acceptance of long-term investment. It is easy to disregard the possibility of making profit even in the first year and yet this has been achieved by a number of recent new product successes.

If, therefore, the need to see the investment as early as possible is accepted, the company should try to begin making profit on a new product in the second year and certainly no later than in the third unless the opportunity is exceptional. The theoretical profit and loss forecasters, who delight in preparing long-term forecasts, showing very large profits after many years following great losses in the first four or five years, may scream at the need for early profits. There will be strong objections that in this way companies cannot maximize opportunities and that it will be impossible to launch any new product. There is certainly some validity in such objections, but on balance they must be outweighed by the advantages of the new attitude.

I am certain that companies must be far more concerned with the short-term profits of a new product if they are to lessen the risks and increase the chances of making money from new products—which must be the main object of the exercise.

The view which the company takes, therefore, of the new product's marketing expenditure at the beginning and in later years must be strongly connected with its desire to see early profit. It follows that the level of expenditure could be cut from that which would have been acceptable previously and even more attention than before will need to be devoted to the way in which the money is spent.

Plate I Advertisement A

"Me, buy a dishwasher?
No thanks!
They're difficult to load...
they don't get the dishes
really clean...and they're
far too big and expensive."

NOT ANY MORE, MADAM!

The all-new KIM Dishwasher has been developed by the precision-minded Swiss to fit real-life kitchens. It loads from the front in exactly one minute. It gets dishes, glasses, cups, knives, forks and spoons, whistling, shiny, clean ... spotlessly dry. And it costs just 69 gns.

They have finally perfected dishwashers. At last it makes sense for you to buy from this investable and merry chore of constant washing-up.

The new KIM dishwasher, after heating the water, will wash and dry the dishes, glasses, cups and cutlery used by six people in eight and a half minutes! And – hold your breath – it will do them so thoroughly and as efficiently as you could do them yourself, even more hygienically.

Designed for real-life kitchens. The new KIM is truly a table-model dishwasher. It measures exactly 19½ inches by 19½ inches. It does not have to be plumbed in. No installation charges. It sits with beautiful compactness on top of your draining board or working surface or, if you prefer, on its own "working space" trolley. It uses the tap in your sink – cold or hot water; for about a minute before you press the button; the tap is then free.

KIM is completely automatic. Here is what you do. Load the dishes, cups, glasses and cutlery into their own specially customised slots. Slide the single rack back into the machine. Close the door. Turn on the tap for a minute. Press the button. Here is what KIM does. Heats the water to 155°F. Mixes in a special detergent. Washes each piece perfectly with a powerful curtain of water. Uses the water twice. Rinses everything with fresh, hot, clean water. Dries contents to a bright sheen. Empties the water into your sink. Shuts itself off.

KIM is more hygienic. KIM uses steaming water to wash up – water at a temperature no human hand could bear yet quite enough for your most delicate glass. KIM does this than water for the rinse. And you need never use a tea towel on your family's dishes again.

KIM is simplicity itself. The engineers have "transformed" dishwashers. They have managed to eliminate all the unnecessary fuss and mess which has tended to make dishwashers so expensive and have developed a precision-minded marvel that is simplicity itself. That's why KIM, the new fully-automatic dishwasher, costs just 69 gns. Or after a down payment of £5, you pay 24 monthly payments of £3.6.6 each.

About the makers of KIM. It took less long years of design, research and testing to produce a dishwasher so practical to KIM. The people responsible are Switzerland's largest manufacturers of fully automatic washing machines and dishwashers. KIM dishwashers are now being manufactured in Britain and are being serviced within hours of your call by a large force of fully-trained British engineers. KIM is completely guaranteed for one year – both parts and labour!

Seeing is believing. KIM is available from the manufacturer. A comprehensive booklet has been prepared which tries to answer any question you can possibly dream up. It shows you KIM in operation. The booklet gives you facts for life and up. Unless you are at least with the idea of washing up for the rest of your life, why not write now. You'll be glad you did.

kim FULLY AUTOMATIC DISHWASHER 69 GNS

Plate II Advertisement B

sixteen   the role of advertising

the difference between good and bad advertising

The increasing need for a company to ensure that it is spending its marketing funds to best effect has already been pointed
out and advertising is in general the most important single
item in that expenditure.

It is also an item which is extraordinarily difficult to measure
in isolation because of all the other variable factors affecting
a new product's sales such as competitive activity, trade reactions, the sales force, display at the point of sale, etc. One is
even tempted to conclude that it does not matter too much
what the advertising is. So long as it is of average competence
and is at the required level of expenditure, its effect will be
relatively constant in helping to sell a certain volume of product in combination with the other forms of marketing expenditure.

Yet nothing could be further from the truth and those who
believe that advertising has an average constant effect and no
more can miss the opportunity of injecting an important advantage into the new product launch. For example, the advertising of Volkswagen in the United States is believed to have
played an important part in establishing it there against the
local competition. Again it is difficult to feel that Schweppes
could have succeeded in the United States without the advertising which features Commander Whitehead in his role of a
typical English gentleman. Similarly the advertising must have
played an important role in the success of such products as
Guinness, Stork margarine and Fairy liquid.

An extraordinary example of the differences between

advertising approaches is provided by advertising for a new dishwasher called Kim. In this case the product was sold direct to the consumer and so the advertising could be judged in isolation from any other factor on the basis of the number of coupons asking for a brochure, resulting directly out of the advertisement. Several advertisements were tested and in one case the same copy was used with two different layouts as illustrated in Plates I and II facing pages 166 and 167.

One would have expected, therefore, that there would be little or no difference in the response to the two advertisements. In practice advertisement A (Plate I) pulled three times more enquiries than advertisement B (Plate II), an amazing performance which can only be attributed to the fact that the public must have found the design in A more pleasing or possibly more noticeable. If it is possible to have such a difference due to change of layout alone, it is feasible to imagine that good, well directed, advertising can benefit a new product to a remarkable extent in comparison with the effect of poor advertising.

Yet the difference between good and bad advertising need not be seen on the creative side alone. Differences in use of the actual media can be just as important. For example, it has been found time and time again that a company buying television time can buy even 15 per cent–20 per cent better than a competitor also using television who does not buy as effectively. This means that careful planning and buying can lead to a saving of £15,000–£20,000 on a budget of £100,000, or even of £100,000 on a budget of £0.5 m. These are saving which can make an important difference to the viability of a new product.

If it is accepted that the difference between good and bad advertising is an important factor in a new product launch and at times can represent the difference between new product failure and success, how does the company determine what is good advertising and what is bad advertising? The old cliché, quoting Lord Leverhulme's remark that half of advertising money is wasted, but one does not know which half, is too close to the truth for comfort even today. Yet the company must make every effort to try to finish up with the best possible advertising, for the rewards are high and so are the penalties for failure.

agency contribution

Because of the importance of advertising in the development of most consumer products, the company needs to choose the advertising agency to handle the product with great care and the decision should be taken at an early stage. Too often the company, having spent years on the development of the product, calls in an agency two or three months before it intends to test market it, so that the agency is faced with a finished product and just needs to add the last ingredient—advertising—in an almighty last-minute scramble.

At times there are circumstances which dictate such unfortunate timing, e.g. if the company suddenly needs to accelerate its plans because of competitive activity, but in general such situations occur because the company does not realize how important the advertising is and what a useful contribution a good agency could make at a much earlier stage.

The possibility of creating advertising at the concept stage, before the product exists, has already been mentioned. Even if there is no need to do this, the agency should ideally be involved in the design of the product, i.e. in the way it is to be presented to the consumer as well as in its naming and packaging. After all, these are parts of the communication process between the company and the consumer which the advertising will later try to foster, so ideally all these elements should fit together. Moreover, if the agency is taken into the company's confidence at an early stage, it will naturally become more involved than it would have been normally and so should make a particularly useful contribution.

If advertising and the agency contribution are so important to a new product, how should a company choose its agency? Very often there is no problem if the company already has an agency working on its existing products, as the new one is simply added to the others.

If, however, there is need to choose an agency—and a company already with an agency should consider the advantages of finding another one for the new product to encourage healthy competition—it is worth while drawing up criteria for selection. At the moment many companies, even large and experienced advertisers, are extremely subjective in this respect and tend to select a small number of agencies of good reputation whom they may ask to make a competitive presentation on the basis of which a decision is made.

This is indeed a strange procedure for choosing a business partner. While the company understands the importance of methodical market studies and research to find a market opportunity, it is prepared to give its advertising to an outside group on the strength of a presentation where there is often a premium on form over content, where the personality of one or two people can be the most important factor. And if the company appoints the agency, the people presenting may be never seen again by the company on a day-to-day basis because they are too busy working on behalf of other companies or presenting to prospective clients!

It seems reasonable that this important decision—the choice of an advertising agency—should be taken only after a systematic process of search and appraisal. I suggest the following procedure:

1. ESTABLISH COMPANY NEEDS

Does the company only want creative work and media buying or does it want outside agency services, e.g. marketing, market research, merchandising, pack design, etc.?

2. ESTABLISH CRITERIA FOR SUITABLE AGENCY

These should, of course, be in line with the company needs. The size of the agency also would need to be considered closely in relation to the likely advertising budget. For example, a budget of, say under £100,000 is unlikely to be very interesting to a large agency who, if it accepts it, will probably put its more junior executives on the account, while it could be one of the more important accounts in a small or medium-sized agency whose top management could well work on it on a day-to-day basis. Moreover it can be agreed that a large established agency has much less incentive than a smaller 'hungry' one. On the other hand a company with a really large budget or one which requires very comprehensive agency services is unlikely to find what it wants in a small or medium agency. In fact it would be unfair to the latter to appoint it and become its dominant client, if there is a need to change to another agency six months later.

3. AGENCY SEARCH

Once the agency criteria are established, it may even be useful to prepare a screening system as for new products, weighting the various factors according to their importance. The company should then consider all the agencies according to the required criteria and it is thought that the large majority can be quickly eliminated mainly on the grounds of size, experience, facilities, or because they handle competitive products.

4. EVALUATION OF SHORT LIST

A short list should be reached and, at a general meeting with each one on the short list, an impression should be formed once the agencies have the opportunity of discussing their past work and results for other companies and of showing the facilities which they can offer. The short list should become shorter as a result and then the company can do much by considering closely the other companies for whom the possible agencies are working and the advertising they are producing. It is always useful to discuss the agencies with one of their current clients who, after all, work with them on a day-to-day basis and so are ideally suited to assess them.

Finally, it would seem useful for the company to send one of its executives to spend a few days with the two or three most likely agencies. In this way he will see them at work for their clients and will be able to assess their faults as well as their good points in normal conditions rather than in the artificial situation of a special presentation which could be most misleading.

I believe that at this stage there should be enough information on which to base a rational decision. At the end of the line the company must choose the most suitable agency for its needs and the choice needs to be a good one. If it is not and if the company needs to make a change too soon, this is harmful to the company and its new product as well as to the agency concerned.

So the most suitable agency is chosen for the new product. The company must now ensure that the right relationship is established. After all, the agency is there to contribute professional expertise in advertising if nothing else, yet advertising is a field where everyone believes he is an expert and there is a strong temptation for companies to offend by dictating what the advertising should be. Sometimes the company will decide what advertising media should be bought against the advice of the agency's media buyer who may have been specializing in media buying for twenty years on behalf of hundreds of companies and who would be the only person really aware of all available media research data. The company can even go as far as to design press advertising layouts or prepare television videotape commercials and hand them over to the agency to complete.

If the company insist on being dictatorial, the advantages of having outside experts are nullified and the agency, even if it continues to work for the company in a slave-like manner, will certainly not be involved in the company's business, so its contribution will be minimal.

It is important, therefore, for the company to recognize the importance not only of advertising but also of the advertising agency and so to choose one which can be treated on equal terms. If the necessary amount of scope is given to the advertising specialists, they will try harder and the company will find a second body of people devoted to the success of the new product. For example, I know of a company which at one time did not even bother to check the advertisements before they went into the media. The managing director said to the agency 'After all, you know what we want to say to our market and you are the experts on how to say it, just go ahead and send me proofs for my files'. This attitude goes too far because the company abdicated its responsibility for final decisions, but it made the agency very conscious of its own responsibility and so the latter approached the advertising with a fantastic devotion, knowing that it was the final arbiter.

the creative policy and execution

All the studies recently conducted in the United States and in the U.K. clearly show that the very large majority of advertisements are completely invisible to the public. We are bombarded by so many advertising messages during the day —on television, in the Press, in the cinema, through the letter box, in the shops—that the chances of any one being seen and remembered by its desired market are extremely slim. It is vital, therefore, that the new product's advertising should be not only persuasive for its particular market but also distinctive, i.e. different enough from the competition to be noticed.

It is essential, therefore, for the agency and company together to hammer out a creative policy concentrating on a specific product advantage and not try to include all the virtues of the new product, so that at the end no single point registers.

For example, when Procter and Gamble launched their new liquid detergent—Fairy Liquid—it could have easily talked about a number of product attributes such as its washing performance, its value for money, its pleasant smell, its convenience, etc. Instead the decision was taken to concentrate all the advertising effort on the point that the product was kind to the housewife's hands, while its other attributes were taken for granted, and the constant repetition of the theme has made an important contribution to the product's success.

Similarly the same company's soap, Camay, obtained an important share of the fiercely competitive soap market through consistent emphasis on its high-priced French perfume. In the toothpaste market one new product would concentrate on decay prevention, another on the product's cleaning properties. In paint, the highly successful Magicote concentrated on the non-drip aspect, while one of the most recent entrants, Crown Plus Two, promoted itself as 'a combination product', i.e. the only paint being both non-drip and hard.

It is necessary, therefore, to establish what are the factors in a new product which the consumer finds important and which would give it an edge over competition. Once this is established—and after all it should stem directly out of the new product development process—this most important selling point should form the foundation of the new product's advertising policy.

Until very recently the United States held a definite lead over the U.K. in the understanding of the need for such concentration on one point. Here, even if the point was established, companies and agencies tended to be nervous to concentrate on it alone and so cluttered the advertising with all the major points, in case any one were overlooked. As a result nothing came across to the consumer.

Now, however, it seems that the situation has changed and the importance of this concentration on one point is recognized. Yet even then there is a gap to be bridged between a strongly concentrated policy and the appropriate creative execution. For example, if it is agreed to advertise a car on its manoeuvrability, it would weaken the advertising if it is found necessary also to include other points in the actual advertising, i.e. that it has much room in the interior or that it is very good quality or that it uses little petrol, etc. If one point is selected, it is normally worth while making a stark advertisement on the one point only. Such concentration is necessary to be noticed among all the advertising messages with which the consumer is being bombarded. Here is the way to more effective advertising.

Concentration of the advertising means that the correct selection of the particular selling point to be promoted is crucial. The initial concept search should serve to indicate the one or more selling points worth building the advertising on. Once the advertising has been prepared, it is normally advisable to validate it by pre-testing it.

advertising pre-testing

If the advertising is important to the success of the new product, as it usually is in the case of consumer products, its impact and suitability should be checked before it appears.

Many companies are reluctant to carry out such research either because of the cost or because, in the pressure of events, there is no time to conduct it and change the advertising if necessary. Although in some cases this attitude is justified, more often than not the pre-test is not considered in relation to the total advertising appropriation. It does not seem reasonable to grudge the cost of pre-testing amounting to, say, £1,000, if the advertising expenditure is £100,000 or £200,000. After all it is logical to assume that the pre-testing should improve the performance of the advertising by 1.0 per cent or by 0.5 per cent respectively.

The actual form of the pre-testing does not matter too much. There are a number of approaches to this type of research which is recognized as one of the most problematical of all and there is no method which does not have some serious disadvantages. Yet, whatever method is used, it should enable the company to decide between two or more advertising campaigns.

Moreover, even if only one solution has emerged for pre-testing, the research will still be most useful, so long as there is enough time to change the advertising if necessary. It is also important for the company to pre-test all its new advertising if the results of research on one campaign only are to be interpreted usefully. A number of companies have accumulated a precious bank of information over the years using a constant research method. In this way a benchmark is available against which every new set of results can be assessed and the relative value of the new advertising can be determined.

seventeen test marketing

the place of test marketing in new product development

Test marketing is normally the last step in the development process before a new product is launched either in a large area or nationally and its role in the step-by-step development approach has already been mentioned briefly.

Whether it takes place at all or at what stage of the process must depend on the financial considerations. If the risk is small, it may be worth dispensing with it. Too often, however, companies make the mistake of proceeding too quickly to a test market as soon as a product is available, without fully realizing that, by doing so, they are making a decision on the viability of the new product, by implying that it is worthy of the expenditure which a test market normally demands.

If the product can be imported or manufactured by another company, the costs of test marketing may not be great, but in most cases a pilot plant is necessary, there are disproportionate costs of research and of production of promotional material and the necessary marketing expenditure is incurred. The average loss per product during the test marketing as calculated by Buzzell and Nourse at $248,000 is an eye opener (see page 194), but even in the U.K. a sum of £50,000 or more for a test market is by no means unusual. The company should consider, moreover, the cost of using the sales force organization in the area to launch the new product, to the detriment of the company's other products, and the risks of poor trade reaction if the product fails.

It is important, therefore, that unless there are special reasons against this policy, by the time the test marketing stage is reached, the product should have passed through enough stages to warrant the expenditure needed in a test market.

There are often strong pressures within the company either to rush through to test market or to dispense with it altogether. The main disadvantage is that it warns the competition and if it is known that competitors are developing similar products or if it is very easy for them to imitate the new one, there is a strong temptation to launch nationally as quickly as possible and thus seek to acquire a lead over competition. This is obviously an important point and there are examples of companies indulging in leisurely test marketing only to be hammered by awake competitors being the first to launch similar products nationally. The success of Alberto Culver in the United States is at least partly attributed to such an opportunistic policy.

Yet it would be wrong to accept too great risks simply because of fear of competition. After all, if a company has settled on a step-by-step development approach culminating in a test market, this means that it has not accepted the risks of a national launch without a test market. Why should this risk be acceptable to the competition? And if the success or failure of the new product depends largely on a few months' lead, the project is surely not a very promising one. One of the factors which the company must have considered from the beginning of the project is competitive action and either the company regards itself superior in marketing terms to the competition or the product advantage it is planning to have will be substantial enough to produce profit for the new product over a number of years. In either case there is no need to panic and take unnecessary risks at the last fence. Even if the competitor decides to go first, this could be an advantage rather than a disadvantage. In practice I have found that rumours about competitive action are rife for years—even three or four years—before the competitor actually is ready and willing to move, so decisions on the basis of such rumours are most unwise.

The arguments for and against the test market must be settled on financial grounds. If the risks are high, it is usually worth while. Or if there is one or a number of factors to be tested, e.g. pricing, weights of marketing expenditure, distribution policies, etc.—which can never be satisfactorily researched except in the market place. If, on the other hand, the marketing costs are relatively low and the major expenditure on plant needs to be incurred before test market or if the product is supplied under licence by another manufacturer, the financial risk of national marketing is small, the risks being really incurred before the test market. In such circumstances there could well be a good argument for a launch in a large area or nationally without any delay in a test market area.

pilot plant operation

The test market for a new product can be held to discover the answer to a number of questions such as:

1 Will the sales force be able to have the time to sell and merchandise the new product?
2 Are the distribution outlets selected the most suitable for the new product and will the trade provide the necessary support?
3 Will the company's organization cope with the new product in terms of production, transport, servicing, etc.?
4 Is it more profitable to sell the product at £25 or £30?
5 Is it more profitable to have marketing support at the rate of £100,000 or of £200,000 nationally?
6 What market share, sales volume and finally profit are likely to be achieved nationally?

In practice a large number of questions such as the above are asked and many test markets are held to answer either one question or a combination of two or more. It is possible, however, to divide the main functions of a test market into two:

a As a pilot plant operation
b To predict level of future performance on a national basis.

The pilot plant function is similar to that in engineering. It is assumed that, however much one plans, there will be unexpected snags in the final plant, so a pilot plant is built, not necessarily as a replica of the full-scale plant but as an approximation so that the engineer can see what the snags are likely to be in practice and can then experiment and decide on the best ways of solving them. Similarly in marketing there can be snags with a new product, particularly in the case of durables which usually have teething problems or if a company enters an unfamiliar field. It is unlikely that all the snags can be foreseen and eliminated in the preliminary planning, so the test market is held for this very purpose.

For example, a new company recently entered a consumer durable field in the U.K. and decided to sell direct to the public. The product was manufactured for them by another company and no experience of direct selling was available, so it was vital to start in an area where the company learnt, largely on an empirical basis, the best method of selling the product, while the organization for manufacturing, delivering and servicing the product was perfected.

Another company had been selling over a long period solely through its own outlets and devised a range of new products to be marketed through outlets other than its own. A test market was held mainly to discover whether it was in fact feasible to obtain distribution in these other outlets over which it had no control.

Finally, a food company entering a new product field was concerned that there could be problems because the new product had shorter shelf life than the other company products. A test market took place, therefore, to see whether the new product could be handled by the existing sales force and distribution arrangements or whether special provisions would be necessary.

In cases where test markets are used for pilot plant purposes they work extremely well and are absolutely invaluable. In fact there is no other way to find the answers to many of the questions raised except in practice, i.e. under market conditions in a limited area.

prediction problems

The majority of test markets, however, are held for predictive purposes and, even in a pilot plant operation, where the activity may bear no comparison with what would be done on a national basis, it is difficult to resist the temptation of calculating the sales and projecting them nationally.

Yet, although there is so much anxiety to predict, there are also important problems in making such predictions. The reasons for these problems are well enough known:

1. There is no area really representative of the whole country. Each one has its own characteristics and companies and their markets have different strengths and weaknesses in different areas.
2. There are differences in the trade structure. In some areas the trade may be controlled by one or two local groups. In others trading organizations from outside the area are important and it may be difficult to obtain distribution in their outlets on a test area basis. In yet other areas the trade may be fragmented among a large number of small companies and businesses. Performance in one of these areas could well be different from what would happen nationally.
3. Competitive action is normally an important factor and there is no control over it. The competition can behave in one way in the test market and in another way on a national basis and this could be enough to make a considerable difference between the two situations.
4. The change in time between test market and national marketing could lead to differences caused by different seasonality, economic conditions, weather, etc. For example, a soft drink test market prediction was completely wrong because of change in the weather which is of course an important factor in this market.

Points such as the above have been recognized for some time and enquiries have been carried out to see whether they in fact affect test market predictions to any degree. Studies in the United States have shown the lack of correlation in many cases between test market and national performance which could not be attributed to changes in a company's marketing policy following the lessons learnt in test market. Strong words have been used, such as, '... traditional market testing has not lived up to its expectations when used as a predictive research tool. The time has come for us to do some serious large scale experimenting with new, and perhaps even dramatic, ways of making this tool more predictive[1]'.

Such opinions were backed by opinion on both sides of the Atlantic. Jack Gold studied U.S. retail audit data for seven established brands in six large areas and the differences between the areas were startling.[2] Assuming that each brand in each area were being test marketed, Gold projected the area sales in each case using three different projection methods, on the basis of the buying income of the population in the area, market shares and comparisons with the leading brands. It was then possible to compare the projections with the actual national sales as measured by the same retail audits and the conclusions were striking and disturbing. When one area projections were used, each area being at least 3 per cent of the United States, in 65 per cent of the projections the error was $\pm$ 15 per cent and in 30 per cent of cases it was over $\pm$ 35 per cent! When combinations of three areas were used for projection, i.e. at least 9 per cent of the United States, the results were more predictable, but even so the error was $\pm$ 15 per cent in 40 per cent of cases. And 15 per cent could well be the margin between success and failure.

Similar analysis has been carried out in the U.K.[3] and again considerable area differences were found. Dr Treasure

1. A. Achenbaum, Address to American Marketing Association, 1964.

2. 'Testing Test Market Predictions', J. Gold, *Journal of Marketing Research, August* 1964.

3. Dr. J. Treasure. Address to Marketing Society, 1964.

'Some Aspects of Test Marketing', P. M. Kraushar, *Advertiser's Weekly,* June 15 1966.

examined two brands. In one case he found that seven times
out of fifteen the error was over $\pm$ 15 per cent. In the other
case it was $\pm$ 15 per cent in fourteen projections out of fifteen.
I have found similar results and in fact one projection I made
was three times the actual figure!

It is not surprising, therefore, that in the last two or three
years there have been serious doubts about the use of test markets for predictive purposes. The analyses of retail audit data
compared projections and actual national sales at the same
period of time, so what could the differences be between one
year and the next? In fact the reason why test markets have
continued to be used where possible was not because companies overcame the doubts but simply because no better
alternatives were found.

A recent Nielsen study[1] has helped to provide more quantitative data on prediction. 141 test markets of packaged goods
in the U.K. and the United States were analysed. 77 of these
went on to national marketing and so it was possible to compare market shares in test market and nationally. When the
average national shares during the first year were compared
with those in test markets, the results were as follows:

All Brands Launched – 77 = 100%	Difference Between National and Test Market Share		
%	%		
28	±5		
21	±6	—	±10
34	±11	—	±20
12	±21	—	±30
5	±31		and over
___			
100			

Thus in almost half the cases the test market share was
within 10 per cent of the subsequent national performance,
i.e. a share of 10 per cent could be assumed to be in the 9 per

1. *Nielsen Researcher*, January/February 1968.

cent–11 per cent range in half the cases. No company could object to such error in prediction. However in 17 per cent of cases the error was over $\pm$ 20 per cent, a margin which would probably be unacceptable. The question which needs to be asked is whether a company would view a margin of error of between $\pm$ 10 per cent and $\pm$ 20 per cent as acceptable for test market projection. If it does, then, on the basis of the Nielsen study, this is likely to happen in over 80 per cent of cases.

A company should certainly build on a safety margin into its profit and loss forecasts and ideally projects should be sought with at least a 20 per cent safety margin. Nevertheless to allow the possibility of up to 20 per cent error for test market prediction alone, when there are so many other factors to be considered, e.g. cost of goods, sales costs, distribution, marketing expenditures, etc., seems high. In practice, I believe that few products can stand a difference of 20 per cent between test market prediction and national performance, although the thought that in half the cases it need not be more than 10 per cent is certainly reassuring.

an approach towards prediction

Whatever the hesitations about predicting test market results, it is obviously necessary to try and in practice good results have been achieved through meticulous planning of the test markets and careful interpretation of the results.

Having made the national marketing plan, it is advisable to prepare a national prediction model to be scaled down to the test area. It is not necessarily scaled down on the basis of population alone as it is important to weight the predictions according to the company's relative strength in the area, the regional pattern for the total market and for competitive brands, etc. Once all the factors are considered and weighted for the chosen test area, the prediction model, covering every period of measurement, could look as follows:

Period	Consumer Awareness	Triers	Regular Buyers	Shop Distri- bution	Sales per shop stocking	Market Shares	Consumer Sales
	%	%	%	%	s.	%	£
1				19			
2	10	2·2	0·7	27	26	4	65,000
3	15	4·5	1·5	29	29	6	82,000
4	18	5·7	1·9	29	25	6	65,000
5	18	6·3	2·1	30	23	5	58,000
6	22	6·9	2·3	31	24	6	65,000
7	26	7·8	2·6	31	26	7	75,000

Such prediction models have a number of important advantages. The main ones are as follows:

1 Careful consideration of all the factors involved in the sales figure—and many more factors could be built in than shown above—must lead to more accurate sales forecasting than if one predicts sales levels only. For example, a sales forecast in a vacuum may seem reasonable until the likely distribution levels and the sales per shop stocking figures necessary to achieve the forecast are considered individually. It is then possible to see, comparing the prediction with the company's own previous experience and with competitive performance, just how reasonable the sales forecast really is.

Moreover the more such prediction models a company makes and sees how they compare with actual results, the more accurate its predictions are likely to be.

2 If each department in the company is consulted on the prediction with which it is particularly concerned, e.g. the sales department on distribution, the advertising department on brand awareness, and the weighting factors provided by the departments are applied in each case, then there should not be any dispute as to the reasons why a test market is doing well or badly. The actual results compared with the predictions accepted in each case will make it clear where are the strong and the weak points in the test markets and there is much less room for argument than is normally the case.

3. The most important advantage stems out of the previous point, i.e. that it is known where the company is doing well and where badly. This means that there is no need to wait till the end of the test market to see what the final sales figures have been and then ponder whether the product is worth marketing in a wider area or not.

If detailed predictions are available for each period, say for every month, during the test market, then it should be possible to make appropriate decisions at an early stage. For example, if by the second month the distribution figures are well below forecast, it is probably worth stopping the test market until the distribution problem is remedied. Or if the proportion of consumers is very low, but, once they try the product, the proportion of them becoming regular users is above forecast, then it may be worth while changing the marketing activity to put emphasis on sampling methods in order to force trial of the product. Again the consumer side of the operation may be poor while distribution and stocks in the trade are good. In that case the consumer acceptance of the product should be reviewed as well as its communication and it may be advisable to stop the test market, change the advertising, and start again if there is nothing wrong with the product.

Thus the advantages of such a process as described above seem clear and work extremely well in practice. They enable the company to achieve above average accuracy in prediction and to use test marketing as a fluid and flexible tool, by treating it as a workshop situation in which it is possible to learn empirically what is the most profitable approach for the product.

area selection

An important part of the process is the selection of the actual test area. Should it be a town, a series of towns, a television area or what?

All the U.S. and U.K. evidence suggests that the larger the area the safer the prediction and it is now generally recognized that individual towns are not useful for predictive purposes. They are extremely suitable, on the other hand, for pilot plant operations, where the size of the area is not important. The only important factor is to have market conditions, whatever the area.

Towns are also used for test markets designed to provide blunt measurement of the relative performance of a particular factor. For example, it should be possible to see whether there is any broad difference in sales of the same product at different prices if it is sold in one town at, say, 1s and in another at 1s 3d. Or the presentation of the product could be tested in two different forms. Or it should be possible to measure the impact of different marketing expenditures, so long as the difference is substantial, say, at the national rate of £100,000 in one town and £250,000 in another well-matched town.

Finally towns can be used as a stepping stone to a larger area test market, in an attempt to minimize the risk of going on at once to a large area. The financial factors and the time involved must be the determining factors in this case, as the time span represented by first a town test and then an area test is likely to be well over a year for most product categories.

Some companies have attempted to use town test markets particularly as saturation tests, i.e. by spending in the test at a considerably higher rate than they could possibly afford nationally, in order to see what market expansion and penetration can be achieved. Such test markets are good in theory, but in practice they are almost impossible to interpret. For example, a company testing a new product in a very large market went into a town and spent at what would be an unaffordable rate nationally to discover that the product obtained an initial share of almost 20 per cent which declined over a number of months to under 10 per cent. As under 5 per cent would have been acceptable anyway, all the company could conclude was that by spending a great deal of money it obtained good results. It was impossible, however, to determine whether the test was good or bad as far as the product was concerned if backed by the planned appropriation nationally and I believe that most saturation tests must finish with such a quandary. It must be preferable to have a rate of expenditure in the area which can be related to national expenditure.

Area tests other than those in towns normally refer to television areas as served by the television contractors. It is rare for a company to consider the area tests in the same context as the town tests. Being much more expensive, they would not be used except for predictive purposes. These, however, are the most common, especially in the case of new products, so if there is a test market for a new product, it would be unusual if it were not held in a television area at some stage.

In theory test areas are selected on the basis of a number of factors such as:

1 Size.
2 Typicality of the consumer.
3 Media facilities.
4 Research services.
5 Typicality of the trade.

In practice, however, selection is normally a matter of elimination and the one or two towns or areas which are left with less negatives than the others are selected. For example, an area where the company is unusually weak or unusually strong is not good for predictive purposes. Then there are some areas where the company cannot obtain adequate distribution—a problem which is becoming more acute as the strength of multiple groups increases. Yet other areas could be rejected for various reasons such as:

1 The sales force are already engaged on other special activities in the area.
2 The area is poorly defined, e.g. the inhabitants shop outside as well as inside the area.
3 There are no suitable media.
4 The company has recently had a failure in the area
5 The market situation is completely atypical.
6 The area is too large.

7 It is so small that it would be dangerous to interpret the results.

Thus in most cases areas are chosen not because of their advantages but because the other areas have even more disadvantages or more serious ones. The various services and facilities which are provided by most of the television contractors and by some of the newspaper groups tend to be incidental and are taken for granted, though they are certainly useful once the area has been chosen.

length of test market

The length of time which a test market needs to last depends very much on the object of the test market and on the market concerned. For example, a pilot plant operation could last only a month or two. For predictive purposes, however, it is normally necessary to wait long enough to be able to measure consumer repeat purchases and this can take a considerable time depending on the frequency of purchase in the market.

It is wrong, therefore, for a company to dictate that the test market must last, say, six weeks or three months if this is too short a time for repeat purchasing to take place, because the results of such a short test could be positively misleading. It is possible that in the initial period all sales are by initial triers and that the product is completely unacceptable so that no one returns. Yet, if not enough time is allowed for repeat purchasing, the test market could be interpreted as a great success on the basis of the initial sales.

The Nielsen study of 141 test markets in the U.S. and the U.K.[1] covered the results achieved during each two monthly period and compared them with the results at the end of the test. It was found that the odds for correctly forecasting the final test results were only 1 in 9 after two months, 1 in 3 after four, 1 in 2 after six, 2 in 3 after eight and 5 in 6 after ten months. As the product categories referred to were all fast-

1. *Nielsen Researcher*, January/February 1968.

moving packaged goods, the importance is underlined of having a test market for at least eight months and preferably longer if predictions are wanted from the test market.

research in the test market

A test market, particularly if conducted for predictive purposes, is by definition a research operation and so provision must obviously be made to obtain the necessary measurements in the area so that the company can interpret the results and have enough information to decide on its action during the test market and after its completion.

The above statement is self-evident, but in practice some companies object to a test market in which the research costs may be the most important single item. Yet wrong economy can and does mean that, having decided to spend, say, £2,000 on research instead of the necessary £3,000 on a test market costing the company, say, £30,000 altogether, the company just cannot interpret the results meaningfully because of lack of information and so the £30,000 is largely wasted.

The research should be linked closely to the prediction models and normally consists of measurement in two areas:

1 The consumer.
2 At the point of sale.

Retail audits to measure consumer sales are rarely enough if they are not supplemented by consumer research into the rate of repeat purchasing. Without such information, the results would be completely misleading, as has already been mentioned.

Companies should also not neglect using their sales statistics to the full. Analysis of trade sales in total can be misleading if sales increase owing to the opening of new accounts and again a constant break out of repeat as against new orders is invaluable in establishing what is really happening in the test market.

eighteen acquisitions

internal or external development

Once the company has spotted a market opportunity, it broadly has the following choices:

1 Internal development.
2 Licensing arrangements or other joint ventures with other companies.
3 Acquisition.

This book has already dealt in some detail with the development of new products through internal sources of the company.

Licensing arrangements with another company are an alternative possibility and some companies have been most successful in obtaining profitable licences, often from overseas, as the Rank Organization with Xerox.

The most common alternative, however, to internal development is clearly acquisition of a suitable company and this method of diversification is very much in vogue at the moment both in the United States and in Europe.

In the U.S. the success of such companies as International Telephone, Litton Industries and Ling Tempco-Vought, which have grown through a programme of constant acquisitions, has been imitated up to a point in the U.K. by, for example, Thomas Tilling and Cape Allman International. Recently the realization that the larger units have a considerable trading advantage has led to an unprecedented number of mergers and acquisitions in some surprising fields, e.g. banks and insurance as well as in cars, T.V. rental, electronics and food. Courtaulds, for example, claim to have taken over 11 companies in 1967 alone and the pace is hotting up.

In 1967 the total value of mergers and acquisitions in the U.K. was about £1,000 m. and in the period January–June 1968 the equivalent figure was already about £1,750 m.

The pace reflects the size rather than the number of the recent bids. Mergers such as those between G.E.C. and A.E.I., British Motor Holdings and Leyland, Radio Rentals and Thorn, Allied Breweries and Showerings, Barclays and Martins Bank, Guardian and Royal Exchange Assurance, Westminster Bank and National Provincial, have pushed into the second rank such mergers as that between Boots and Timothy Whites which in rationalizing the total retail structure in the U.K. chemist trade would normally have been one of the more important commercial events in any one year.

The U.S. companies are also very active, although their growth as one of the most potent economic forces in Europe will probably be inhibited in the short term by financial restriction recently imposed on them. Many of the largest U.S. corporations have been extremely busy, especially on the Continent, in buying up local companies to obtain a foothold or consolidate their current business there and it is forecast that by 1982 U.S. industry in Europe will be the world's greatest industrial power after the U.S.A. and Russia.[1]

Within the United States acquisitions have presented probably the fastest method of growth for a large number of companies. For example, according to the Federal Trade Commission[2] the fifty largest food manufacturers in the U.S. bought some 985 companies between 1950 and 1965, i.e. over one a year on average! According to the Commission the declining number of food manufacturers in the U.S. and the fast-rising trend in diversification among the larger companies are closely related to this merger activity.

It is also noteworthy that, whereas at one time only a certain

1. *The American Challenge*, J. J. Servan-Schreiber, Hamish Hamilton, 1968.
2. *The Structure of Food Manufacturing*, Technical Study No. 8, U.S. Government Printing Office, 1966.

number of firms looked towards acquisition as a normal commercial technique, in recent years this attitude has spread to the majority of companies. Thus, as Louis Stern has pointed out,[1] companies which in the past have depended entirely on growth from within have ventured into the acquisition field, e.g. Hersey Chocolate which recently bought San Georgio Macaroni Company or Ralston-Purina which merged with Van Camp Sea Food Company in 1963. Similarly in Europe every type of company seems on the lookout for acquisitions either for offensive or for defensive purposes. For example, the French biscuit industry was highly fragmented among a large number of companies only a few years ago, but felt it necessary to merge into a small number of large units to combat the U.S. companies entering the market. In the same way the biscuit market in the U.K. has become rationalized through mergers into two large groups—United Biscuits and Associated Biscuit Manufacturers—which between them dominate the market.

The advantage and disadvantage of acquiring a company instead of internal development need to be considered carefully and much will depend on the market concerned and on the developing company's attitude and organization. The following factors should be considered in this context:

1 Experience of the market in which an opportunity has been found.
2 R and D experience of the above market.
3 Technical R and D facilities.
4 Time when profits are needed from project.
5 Liquid or share capital available for acquisition.
6 Existence of suitable companies to be acquired.
7 Balance between risk and opportunity of both internal development and acquisition.

If the company has the facilities and experience to develop from within, it is often more profitable to do so.[2] Even if the

1. 'Acquisitions. Another Viewpoint', Louis W. Stern, *Journal of Marketing*, July 1967.
2. 'Growth from Within May Pay Off Faster', *Business Week*, September 17 1966.

suitable experience is missing in many cases the company can easily recruit one or two individuals with the necessary skill and build the R and D effort round them. Such an attitude requires, however, senior and middle management to have a broad and flexible outlook towards marketing so that they are able to market successfully products in unfamiliar fields, especially in companies where management have been with the company for many years and so there is little experience of working in other companies and other fields.

Moreover, the cost as well as the time necessary for internal development of new methods should not be underestimated. An interesting study[1] in the U.S. by Buzzell and Nourse on behalf of the Grocery Manufacturers of America calculated that in the period 1954–64 nineteen grocery manufacturers spent on average $94,000 per new product on product research and development and on marketing research before test marketing. During test marketing the average loss based on 72 new products was $248,000 per product and in addition capital plant investment, often substantial, needed to be added. If the products were launched broadscale, marketing expenditures per product averaged $1.4 m. in the first year and $950,000 in the second, so that by the end of the third year only 61 per cent of the new products had broken even on a cumulative basis without allowance for the initial capital investment.

Although no equivalent figures are available for the U.K., the U.S. findings by Brizzel and Nourse certainly seem close to what needs to be spent on an important new product in the U.K.

It is clear, therefore, that internal development can be expensive, risky and certainly takes time, although in the long term the opportunity is greater, if the product succeeds, than it would be through acquisition which would normally involve an already established product at a certain stage of market

1. *Product Innovation. The Product Life Cycle and Competitive Behaviour in Selected Food Processing Industries*, R. D. Buzzell and R. E. M. Nourse, Arthur D. Little Incorporated, 1966.

development. On the other hand acquisition seems safer as it concerns established products, but requires capital and often provides more modest growth opportunities.

In general it is unlikely that a company should consciously choose to grow either by acquisitions or internal development alone, whatever the market. Internal development tends to be a continuous process, certainly in the fields in which the company is already operating and in others in which it feels it can develop new products, whereas acquisition would be considered in specific cases, if there is a market opportunity which the company cannot exploit otherwise, if there is need to accelerate the company growth and capital is available and if there is a suitable company to acquire which fits in with the operation.

dangers of acquisitions

There is no doubt that while in the United States the Anti-Trust regulations make further mergers in many industries difficult, in Europe the trend for more and more mergers will continue. The breaking down of national frontiers within the Common Market and the possibility that the number of countries within the Common Market will soon increase will lead to an even greater realization of the need of large industrial units to tackle what has become and will be the huge European market.

In the U.K. there is considerable pressure both in industry and in government towards further mergers, very much encouraged by the State-aided Industrial Re-organization Corporation which has helped to bring about a number of mergers, including recently the G.E.C.–A.E.I. one and which is actually canvassing the formation of large units to be a force in Europe. Neddy and various ministries are also trying to stimulate mergers and it was noteworthy that at the beginning of 1968 Prof. Blackett, President of the Royal Society and Deputy Chairman of the Ministry of Technology's Advisory

Council on Technology, publicly praised the number of mergers which had suddenly developed and hoped that there would be even more.

It is evident that the current trend regarding mergers can be beneficial. The relatively low productivity in the U.K. has been often attributed to the very marked fragmentation of U.K. industry, so the larger units should compete more efficiently with overseas companies operating both in the U.K. and abroad.

The picture, however, is by no means as clearly black and white as the above analysis suggests and it is possible that the profitability of the larger unit becomes smaller than the total of the constituent companies if run individually.

A recent study[1] of 186 U.K. companies over the period 1954–63 shows that the largest companies are the most unprofitable. Those with assets of over £15 m., which means that they would be in the list of the largest 300 U.K. companies, had an average pre-tax return on assets of 14.6 per cent over the ten-year period. Companies with net assets between £1 m. and £15 m. earned an average of 16.4 per cent and those under £1 m. 18.3 per cent.

It is dangerous, therefore, to represent mergers as the answer to every problem and so persuade a company's management that, if they have a problem or if they just want to grow, the automatic solution is a merger. It is easy to imagine that a company's management would decide that they must merge, whatever the circumstances, without thinking about the reasons for the merger, the characteristics of the other company or the subsequent circumstances. It is not surprising that Industrial Mergers state that almost 80 per cent of the 400 companies interested in acquisitions on their register have only vague policies or no policies at all for development.

It is vital, therefore, that companies should not yield to such 'merger hysteria' which can lead to severe problems and to disasters. And there are clear indications that there have been

1. J. M. Samuels and D. Smyth, Birmingham Graduate Centre for Management Studies. *Economia*, June 1968.

a number of such failures both in the United States and in Europe.

Booz Allen and Hamilton analysed 120 U.S. acquisitions in their 1965 new product study. They discovered that 64 per cent of the acquisitions were considered good, 25 per cent doubtful and 11 per cent had been sold again or liquidated subsequently. Thus over one third of the acquisitions were claimed to be poor or doubtful by executives in the acquiring companies, some of whom would be reluctant to admit that an acquisition had been disappointing. It can be safely assumed, therefore, that in reality well over a third, possibly about a half of the acquisitions had been either doubtful or failures.

It is noteworthy that the Booz Allen study suggests that companies learn from experience of acquisitions and that those which have made a number are more likely to be successful than those for whom this is an unusual occurrence. Thus 30 per cent of the companies which had made at least five acquisitions claimed that their last acquisition had been poor or doubtful, while the equivalent figure for companies who had made only one or two acquisitions was 46 per cent.

John Kitching,[1] in his recently completed study in the United States, carried out depth interviews with senior executives of 22 companies who had altogether been involved in 181 mergers during the period 1960–65 and so at least two years had since elapsed when their merit could be carefully assessed. Almost half of the mergers were found to be conglomerates and as many as 42 per cent of these were considered to have been failures. On the other hand only 11 per cent of the horizontal mergers were considered failures—a comparison which shows clearly the dangers of entering a field which has no connection with a company's existing markets.

It is believed that the proportion of conglomerate mergers is considerably smaller in Europe than in the United States. For example, a recent analysis of seventy-four large mergers which took place in the U.K. in the period March–May 1967 showed

1. 'Why Do Mergers Miscarry?', J. Kitching, *Harvard Business Review*, November/December 1967.

that as many as seventy covered companies in the same product range as the purchaser and this pattern has not changed during the rest of 1967 and during 1968.

Yet even if the proportion of conglomerates is very small in Europe, it is clear that many mergers are unsuccessful. In a study published at the end of 1967 [1] mergers completed in the U.K. during 1965 were examined and profits before and after the mergers were compared. In 1965 42 per cent of the take-over companies concerned showed a profit increase of more than 20 per cent over 1964 and only 12 per cent had lower or static profits. In 1966, however, the position was quite different. As many as 38 per cent of the companies showed no profit growth over the previous year.

Even if the difficulties in the U.K. economy during 1966 affected the profits of the companies involved in the study, the main reason must have clearly been the unsatisfactory nature of the mergers, at least in the short term.

why some mergers fail

It is difficult to classify a merger as a failure as what seems a failure to the outsider could in fact be a success, according to the original criteria set for the operation. Moreover a merger which leads to poor results initially could prove most profitable in the long term.

Nevertheless the evidence already discussed clearly shows that many mergers do fail. Why?

There are many reasons, often depending on the companies or on the personalities involved when two companies decide to join forces. The main reasons, however, appear to be the following:

1. POOR OR INSUFFICIENT PLANNING

In the United States many companies go through a very thorough and lengthy planning process starting with a statement of objectives and going on to detailed examination of

1. *Management Today,* November 1967.

both markets and companies before a bid is normally made. Kitching's study clearly showed the importance of experience of acquisitions and companies without such experience should be even more insistent on thorough planning as a substitute for such experience.

After all, if it is accepted that a considerable amount of planning is necessary for a company to launch a new product, the same argument applies, only to a very much greater degree, in the coming together of two companies with different managements, personnel and procedures as well as with different products.

The financial implications of a merger are in fact normally considered with some care by the company and by its financial advisers and the terms are usually determined on the basis of a study of the balance sheets. Where many companies fail, however, is in consideration of the marketing implications of the merger. It seems natural that questions should be asked such as:

1 What is the market potential for the product range which is being added by the new company in relation to the existing range?
2 What happens if one sales force handles both companies' products or is it better for both sales organizations to continue?
3 What are the possible savings in distribution to the trade?

Yet such questions are often not studied in detail either because a decision needs to be made fast or because it is felt that to answer them it would be necessary to bring in a large number of executives with the resulting danger of a breach of security or simply because the importance of the marketing implications is just not appreciated.

It is not surprising, therefore, that a number of deals based on study of balance sheets alone turn out to be disastrous. For example, a number of acquisitions have taken place where a large company bought a much smaller one, the price being based on the assumption that the smaller company's sales could be increased substantially once they were handled by a large sales force. This can be a doubtful assumption and it has happened more than once that the smaller company's sales not only did not increase but in fact declined following the takeover, because products which had been vital to a small sales force became unimportant to a large sales force selling many high volume lines. In some cases it was also found subsequently that, even if there seemed scope to increase distribution, the small company's lines had in fact reached saturation in their outlets, e.g. it is absurd to consider that non-food products have potential for 100 per cent distribution in grocers.

One of the larger U.K. consumer goods companies made a very important acquisition recently and paid a high price mainly based on the assumption that the two companies had mostly the same customers in the trade and so very large savings in distribution costs would result. It was a reasonable assumption as the companies were both in the same type of outlet, yet what would have been a simple check of the two companies' records was not carried out and it was only after the takeover had taken place that it was realized that the assumption was not founded on fact. The two companies had unexpectedly little overlap in distribution and so the planned savings in transport did not materialize!

Another acquisition of a small regional company marketing short shelf-life foods within a small radius of its factory was made on the extraordinary basis that, following the takeover, marketing funds would be injected to expand the operation and that the profit picture would be projected in direct proportion to the geographical area covered. It did not take long to find out, after a handsome price had been paid for the company, that it was possible to expand the geographical radius of what had been a very profitable operation when it covered a small area. Neither the products nor the organization were suitable for a larger operation.

Many other fatal examples can be quoted—of companies which after takeover were found to market unacceptable products—of companies depending on one man who left after the takeover so that the companies collapsed immediately—of companies whose management had pushed up profits to the utmost immediately before selling and whose profit peak could not be maintained in the long term.

Yet what is self-evident, even if one talks from hindsight, is the ease with which many of the assumptions could have been checked beforehand and quickly. Very few companies seem to understand the importance of studying the marketing implications of a merger and their financial advisers, such as merchant banks, are rarely equipped to appreciate this problem.

2. LITTLE MANAGEMENT CAPACITY

In some cases it is planned to integrate the two companies after the merger. In other cases the intention is to keep the two operations separate, the link being mainly a financial one. Quality of management is particularly sought, so that the company which has been taken over can continue to function as before under the same good management.

Yet it is largely a myth to suppose that the acquiring company's management, having negotiated the deal, can then continue to look after their existing company and simply wait for the money to roll in from the other one without spending any time on the management of the latter.

Experience of mergers on both sides of the Atlantic clearly shows the need for considerable management time after the merger as well as before it. It is unrealistic to believe that the company which has been taken over can carry on as if nothing had happened, as their management's incentives must have changed.

Either their management is so good that it is advisable to integrate it within the structure of both companies and it is not unusual for an executive of a company which has been taken over to emerge at the top of both companies eventually. Alternatively the acquired company's management is not up to the mark and so their role is partly or wholly replaced by the company taking over.

In either case the management of the latter needs to spend considerable time in directing the communication and integrating between the two companies and failures take place if management has not planned for this activity or does not have time to carry it out.

3. CONGLOMERATES

In the United States, experience of conglomerate mergers has shown that they can lead both to great failures and to great successes. The growth of Litton Industries and Ling Tempco-Vought has been breathtaking, but at the same time this type of company seems particularly subject to great profit fluctuations as the recent profit fall of Litton Industries has shown. Litton has become an empire covering manufacture and marketing of over 9,000 different products and has become involved in almost everything from space probes to typewriters. Yet in the six months up to February 1968 its profit dropped by 30 per cent. Why?

The answer probably goes back to the principles of a conglomerate. It is essential to have a high stock market valuation in relation to earnings so that the company's assets can be used in taking over other companies with its highly-valued shares. The financial assets of the companies taken over can normally be rearranged then and the high price/earnings ratio has a snowballing effect on the acquisitions.

Thus the conglomerate operator buys fast and continuously —it is estimated that 70 per cent of all mergers in the United States in the period 1960–67 were conglomerates—and buys in unrelated industries on the assumption that good management methods apply whatever a company's field of operation, so that the same team can manage any type of company.

The above assumption is vital to the success of a conglomerate because the latter must depend on continuing success to hold its stock market image and thus be able to acquire more companies. Yet there are indications that, although the same management methods can be adapted to many industries, each industry has its own expertise and it is unreasonable to expect one team to be as good in each industry as a good team experienced in that particular industry.[1]

It is clear, therefore, that conglomerate mergers are particularly risky and the study by John Kitching certainly supports this view. If this is true of the United States, it is even more true of Europe where management techniques are on the whole less advanced and where there are very few companies really equipped to deal with the problems as well as with the opportunities of a conglomerate merger. Let me quote the President of Du Pont on the subject: 'Running a conglomerate is a job for management geniuses, not ordinary mortals like us at Du Pont.'

Yet the dangers of a conglomerate merger are often not recognized and companies go ahead without appreciating what is really involved. It is hardly surprising, in the circumstances, if there are so many failures when a company, in addition to the normal problems of merging with another company, also has the task of dealing with completely unfamiliar markets and does not even appreciate the problems. The nearer the merger is to the company's experience, the safer the merger.

how to approach a merger

Although many mergers fail, a sense of balance needs to be preserved and the advantages in certain situations of considering a merger or an acquisition instead of internal development need to be borne in mind. It is vital, however, that the merger should be studied as an integral part of the company's development policy and not as a haphazard unrelated activity simply arising because a company may be available for buying. The acquisition should come as a result of a set development policy leading the company to specific market opportunities

1. 'The Perils of the Multi-Market Corporation', *Fortune,* February 1967.

which are better exploited by acquisition than through internal development. At the same time flexibility needs to be preserved with any such process and an opportunity could arise if a company is suddenly found to be interested in a takeover. If this happens, the takeover simply needs to be related to the company's development policy and should be compared with the other possible opportunities facing it. Thus the two processes can be illustrated as follows:

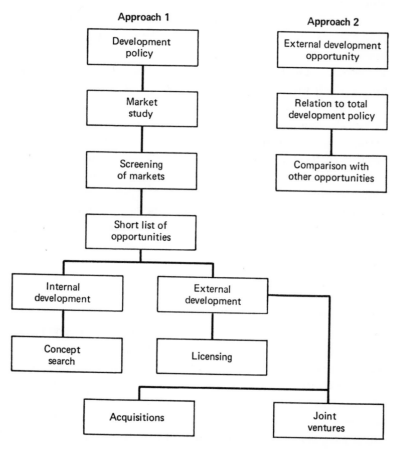

Whichever the process, it is important to set out in advance the criteria required for the company to be taken over, which can be used as a basis for a screening system designed to differentiate between the various companies in the market. If the company is known to be available, it is still advisable to consider it in relation to the others as a better opportunity may present itself. If, on the other hand, it is necessary to find out what companies are available, it is worth while to do so at a relatively early stage, because time and money would be wasted if a very full study were carried out leading to perhaps one company which is then found to be uninterested or unavailable.

In practice it should be possible to make a short list of say 10–15 companies which look the most promising in relation to the required criteria and to approach them informally, in order to see whether they are interested or not in takeover in principle. Then, after eliminating those obviously not interested, the company can concentrate its attention on the others and finally decide on the most suitable one among them, with regard both to the financial and to the marketing implications.

The kind of process described above, relating the merger to a company's resources and policies, should cut down the number of failures and ensure that the mergers which take place are profitable ones. Such an approach is going to become particularly important because as the concentration of power in all consumer goods fields increases, so there will be fewer and fewer small- and medium-sized companies. It is likely that the large majority of these companies will be taken over and so more and more often a company will be tempted to buy another one for no other reason than because it is the only one left in the field! Yet competition to buy the few companies left in particular markets is likely to benefit only the companies being taken over unless the decisions are taken analytically and not emotionally. The most successful companies will be those which will resist the temptation of taking over companies for the wrong reasons and which will see that, unless acquisition of another company can make an important contribution, internal development is likely to be a more profitable course.

nineteen conclusion

It all sounds reasonable on paper, but does it work? The test of the approach towards new products and diversification as described in this book is whether a company adopting it is more successful than it would be otherwise.

I hope that my conviction has come through that the approach itself is not and cannot be a magic formula for success. There is no substitute for creative ideas. If these exist, however, it is most important that the company should have a policy and a set of procedures to sort out the most suitable ideas for the company and to progress them successfully.

Although there is usually a wide gulf in business between theory and practice, there is nothing in this book which is not already practised by a number of companies on both sides of the Atlantic. Unfortunately in the U.K. such companies are very few, many of them being U.S. subsidiaries in this country. In my experience, the small group of companies with a disciplined approach to development and diversification, who are also not afraid to be flexible enough to learn from their mistakes and who regard decision and risk taking as normal business practice, are streaking ahead of the mass of U.K. companies who still find it hard to adapt their management attitudes and their organization to this challenge. The next few years will show whether the latter companies will recognize their problems fully and so will change or whether they will be left behind and eventually probably become absorbed by the more successful ones.

index